THE SANTEE DELTA

WATERS & VOICES

BOB RAYNOR

Published by Evening Post Books, Charleston, South Carolina

Copyright © 2023 by Bob Raynor

All rights reserved.

First edition

Editor: John M. Burbage and Elizabeth Hollerith
Designer: Aren Straiger/Design4One

A previous version of "Tale of the two great canoeists" was first published in South Carolina Wildlife in 2016.

No part of this book may be reproduced or transmitted in any form or by any means, electronic or mechanical, including photocopying, recording or by information storage and retrieval system – except by a reviewer who may quote brief passages in a review to be printed in a magazine, newspaper, or on the web – without permission in writing from the publisher. For information, please contact the publisher. First printing 2023 Printed in the United States of America

ISBN: 978-1-929647-79-8

Contents

Preface i
Prologue 1
Chapter 1 The Prehistoric Delta 5
Chapter 2 The Command of Water 15
Chapter 3 Wambaw 33
Chapter 4 Terror and Death in the Delta 51
Chapter 5 Women of Hampton 63
Chapter 6 Tale of the Two Great Canoeists 77
Chapter 7 Swimming the Santee 85
Chapter 8 They Changed the River 91
Chapter 9 Protecting the Delta 103
Epilogue 121
Notes 133
Acknowledgments 151
Illustration Credits 155
Bibliography 159
Index 169

To the next generation

Sully, Seabrook, Claudia, and Sunny

Preface

Starting in 2005, I looked across from the North Point of Cape Island at the next island to the north, Murphy, and beyond to Cedar Island. The viewpoint from Cape Island was near a specialized nursery, the Cape Romain National Wildlife Refuge loggerhead turtle nest protection program hatcheries, which I had helped build annually. The north end of Cape Island consisted of sandy beaches, dune fields, and salt marshes. Murphy Island had a greater range of habitats: its maritime forest stretched close to the shore of Alligator Creek, separating Murphy from Cape Island, and out of view was an extensive watery world of impoundments. Cedar Island, appearing to the north, was one more intriguing attraction.

While involved in a project to explore all of the islands large and small in Cape Romain, it was natural to continue on with Murphy Island as part of that effort. One unplanned result was the discovery of the Santee Delta, what turned out to be a separate and much larger project. Unconsciously I became a student of the Santee Delta. There was no syllabus for this course, and I have ambled along in this study for over a decade. It became evident that the Santee Delta is an area rich in natural and human history, and encompasses a depth of complexity and dynamics not easily uncovered. The trajectory of this study did not proceed linearly, but branched off into wider fields.

How does one describe the character of a place? The waters impacting and transforming the Santee Delta, flowing downstream from the upcountry and rolling in from the Atlantic, stood out as elemental forces to examine. These waters are the source for the rich and diverse ecosystems and associated wildlife. The people of the Delta, including residents, property owners, and visiting travelers, added their voices to the telling of the story. The perspectives of visitors became important sources for the narrative. While some of these voices have received a wide audience due to their written work, accessing others has been more difficult.

What methods are most beneficial to get at the Delta's essence? I have, for the most part, departed from the practice of my two previous books, in which I constructed the narrative from my explorations utilizing a small sailboat; the Delta's story required a different tack. Pertinent books about the area, as well as more peripheral works, formed a broad reading list. The fields of biography, genealogy, history, botany, ecology, geology, and archaeology contributed to the study. My interest in cartography inspired a wide examination of historic maps, surveys, and plats. Among the readings, historic correspondence was particularly instructive. For the unlettered, the aforementioned correspondence and other written work provided information from the point of view of the writer. Recorded actions and behavior added insight into the thoughts and beliefs of people who did not leave a written record.

It was important to wander from the Delta in telling the story, and roam in its immense watershed. What happened upriver on the Santee had a great impact on the Delta. A Lowcountry tributary emptying into the Delta, Wambaw Creek, contains a wealth of natural and cultural history, and I admit to straying out of the geographic Santee Delta to explore the Wambaw. The Santee Delta and its history cannot be understood without a full consideration of the powerful forces impacting the Lowcountry and South Carolina: slavery and the slave trade, immigration, the Revolutionary War, the Rice Kingdom, the Civil War, the Great Depression, the New Deal, and "carpetbagger conservation."

One method of researching the Santee Delta became a project in itself. In searching out living people who could share their memories and experiences living and working in the Delta, I identified a number of good candidates. The importance of recording their interviews justified developing this effort as an oral history project, *Voices of the Santee Delta*. Two sponsoring organizations, the South Carolina Historical Society and the Village Museum, shared the support; financial assistance was awarded from South Carolina Humanities. The Lowcountry Digital Library at the College of Charleston became the repository and access point for these interviews, including audio, abstracts, searchable transcripts, and photos.

Readers may turn to the archived interviews of *Voices of the Santee Delta*, and listen to audio files of those voices by searching the digital library for the *Voices of the Santee Delta* oral history project collection. This oral history project provided an in-depth and diverse approach to understanding the Santee Delta. The undertaking also enabled me to develop relationships that facilitated the research. I have drawn on these people after the oral history project concluded.

As in my previous works, I used my investigations on the ground and on the water. Initially, I ventured out on my sailboat *Kingfisher* from McClellanville on long sails through Cape Romain to Murphy Island. As I began to understand the breadth of the Delta, I also used the public landings at the Pole Yard on the North Santee and the South Island Ferry Landing on the Intracoastal Waterway. Canoes were convenient for other trips. I accompanied others on boating excursions into the interior of Murphy Island. In all of these experiences, I followed sailors and paddlers who had traveled these waters. And where access was possible, I walked throughout the public lands: Santee Coastal Reserve, Santee Delta Wildlife Management Area, Hampton Plantation, Washo Reserve, the beaches of Murphy and Cedar Islands, and Francis Marion National Forest.

I participated in several projects in the Santee Delta as a volunteer. In 2016, I joined staff and volunteers with The Nature Conservancy in replanting cypress trees in the Washo Reserve. I also participated as a volunteer in archaeological investigations at Hampton Plantation State Historic Site.

Early on, I accepted that I could tell only part of the story, and the work would not be encyclopedic. I was composing a portrait of the Santee Delta. There are other people, events, and places worthy of consideration in studying the Delta. This acceptance was not only about the narrative's limits but also acknowledgment of the depth of the Delta's natural world and human stories.

Despite all my efforts, lingering questions remain to which the Delta has not divulged its answers. These mysteries and hidden worlds contribute to the allure of this Lowcountry place. New researchers and methodologies will surely bring more answers to light in the coming years. The Delta's phenomenal landscape, wildness, and cultural heritage will inspire future explorations and study.

Bob Raynor
Awendaw, South Carolina
July 2022

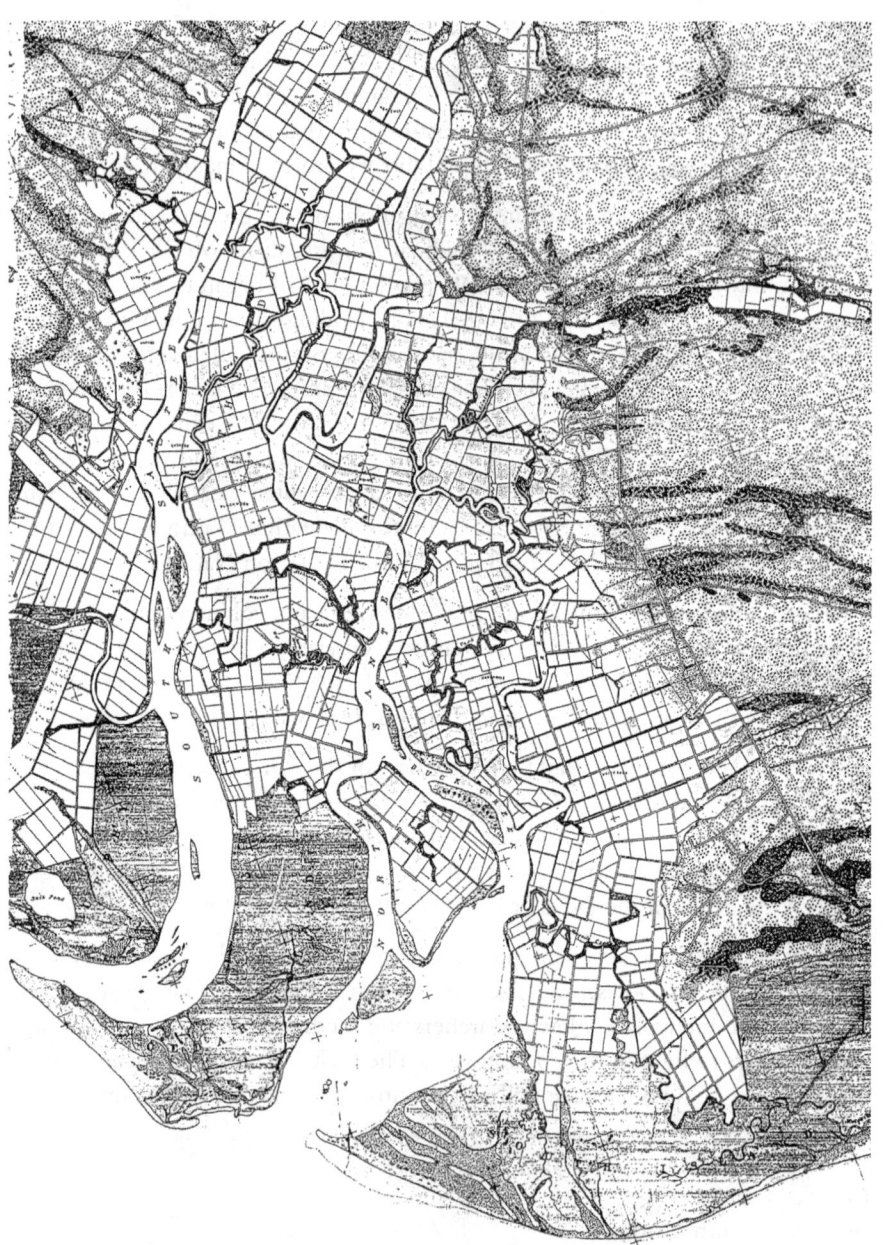

Santee River Coast Survey of 1875, illustrating the Santee Delta's hundreds of diked rice fields.

Prologue

The distant waters of the Santee seep, murmur, surge, cascade, and merge in a multitude of streams flowing from the Blue Ridge to the rolling Atlantic.

The Carolinas' terrains dictate the waters' trajectories, rushing down mountains and continuing at a lively pace through the Piedmont. The Santee system has no single source but is dendritic, with capillaries networked into arteries. As the combined waters swell, they acquire names, some voiced in antiquity and reaching the present. Smaller watercourses become rivers: Enoree, Tyger, Green, Reedy, Saluda, Pacolet, Linville, Catawba, and Broad. Near the fall line, the multiple streams combine into two main rivers, Wateree and Congaree, and further join in the coastal plain to form the Santee. The land again changes the character of the channel, now meandering through the flatlands in a sinuous path. Water originating in the Appalachians approaches a fork only a few miles from the Atlantic. The waters diverge north and south of the massive sediment accumulation, the great river's delta. Those two watercourses split again closer to the ocean and then rejoin before emptying into the Atlantic. For ages, the Santee's floodplain has drained a massive area: 40 percent of South Carolina and a sizable section of North Carolina. The waters of the Santee reveal the Carolinas' geodiversity: cascading over falls and fall line rapids; sauntering along the coastal

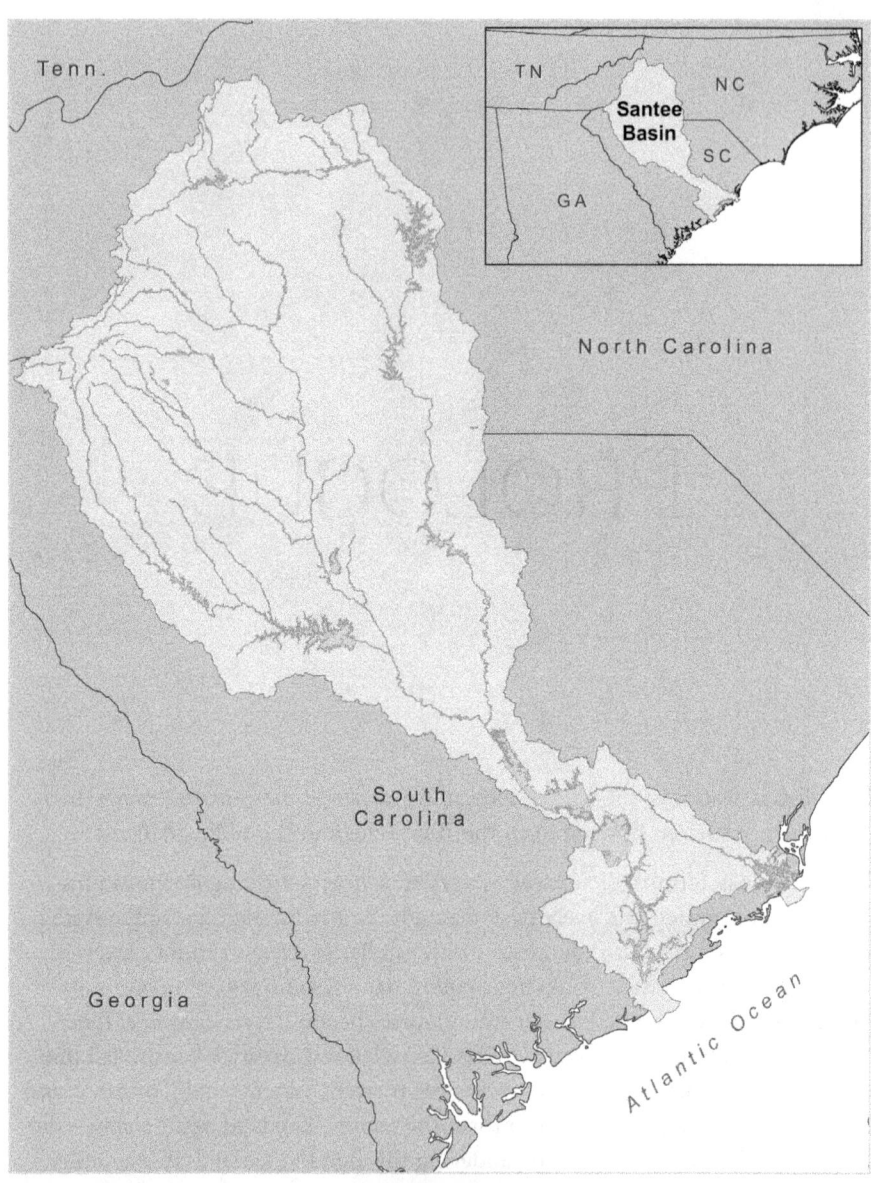

The Santee River basin in South and North Carolina, illustrating the enormous watershed.

plain; and dumping sediments on the floodplain, the Santee Delta, the barrier islands, and offshore shoals.[1]

Twice a day the salt waters of the incoming tides push back at the two inlets, the North Santee and the South Santee. These gaps in the barrier islands can best be described as outlets for the river's discharge into the ocean. The river's pulse for eons has confined the saltwater's effect along the immediate coastal strand and estuary. The tidal interaction between the fresh and salt waters has impacted the Santee Delta's ecosystems. The salt waters would bring the influences of the Atlantic world, and the movement of people from Europe and Africa.

People have traveled the waters of the Santee Delta for thousands of years. The shell middens, prehistoric household debris piles, mark the camps of seasonal foragers who headed downstream through the Delta[2] to coastal marine food resources. Larger canoes probably came later from the paramount chiefdom Cofitachequi on the Wateree, paddling on voyages of trading, slaving, and possibly tribute collecting from the smaller coastal tribes. The return journey involved a difficult paddle against the river's current, or alternatively by foot on a trail later known to European settlers as the Great Catawba Trading Path.[3]

The anonymity of these indigenous canoeists leaves considerable gaps in our understanding of these peoples. Even John Lawson, the noted explorer and chronicler of Native Americans, on his journey in 1701 mentioned "three Indian Men and one Women, that had piloted the Canoe from Ashly-River" without giving their names. Upon leaving them after departing the home of "Mons. Eugee," they had hired "a Sewee-Indian, a tall lusty Fellow," to continue the trip overland. Lawson only included his name, Scipio, in his journal as they voyaged on without him, but he did mention several attributes of this Native American. Scipio carried their clothes in a pack of great weight, and despite his burden, they had a difficult time keeping up with his pace. When Scipio ferried the party for a few miles on the Santee River, Lawson observed they would have been cast off if not for the Sewee Indians "who are excellent Artists in managing these small Canoes."[4]

The peoples plying these waters were of three continents. Diseases decimated the indigenous inhabitants in the Santee Delta, and some of the survivors relocated inland to assimilate with other groups like the Catawba. Europeans recognized the spiritual and physical importance of the rivers in the Indians' lives. Santee, the name of a tribe farther up the river, remained after the disappearance of this indigenous group and the death of their language. Europeans came to the Delta, notably the French Huguenots who settled on the lands along the Santee. Some of these early Huguenot settlers probably paddled, rowed, and sailed on the Delta's waters, including Daniel Huger, Elie Horry, Barthélémy Gaillard, and Isaac Mazyck. The colonists gradually increased their workforce with enslaved peoples from another continent, Africa. Captives of the West African slave depots stretching from Senegal to Angola—Gorée, Bunce Island, Cape Coast Castle, Mina, Annamaboe, and other slave "factories"—crossed the Atlantic Ocean by the infamous Middle Passage to Charleston, prior to embarking on travel to the plantations of the Santee Delta. These Africans and their languages were diverse, including Wolof, Malinke, Mandinka, Fula, Mende, Twi, Fante, Ewe, Fon, Yoruba, Hausa, Ibo, Efik, and Kongo. Africans arriving in the Lowcountry spoke forty to fifty languages, and the need for communication helped to forge a new creole language, Gullah.[5]

We know about the people from Africa traveling on the waters of the Santee Delta mainly from the writings of people of European descent. These African Americans would become the majority population, at times making up around 90 percent of the Delta's people. Partial stories of the enslaved come to us from the eighteenth and nineteenth centuries. A newspaper advertisement tells us of Jack, a boatman and pilot from one of the Horry plantations, taking off in a canoe to make a perilous journey to escape bondage. Another group of enslaved people owned by Harriott Pinckney Horry returned from Murphy Island after burying the victims of an 1822 hurricane. An owner shipped two slaves to Georgetown for sale; these enslaved men were newly arrived from Africa and made an unsuccessful attempt at escape from Wambaw Plantation. They may have met a boatman named Abram, who had the same owner; Abram's occupation allowed him some limited liberty traveling between Wambaw and Charleston.[6]

The enslaved Africans of the Santee Delta have found a voice in their descendants. The veils of history and racism have lifted to reveal their lives and communities. A light has shone on some noteworthy individuals, including a Guardian Angel. The interest of a wider community has spurred the recording of the voices of others, and their stories have become an essential element of the Delta. The richness of the Delta's history comes to life in the tales of individual men and women: free and enslaved, Loyalist and Patriot, resident and visitor, and indigenous and otherwise.

The Santee Delta remains to a great extent a hidden world. For the uninformed traveler driving across the physical Santee Delta, and over the bridges crossing the North and South Santee Rivers, the landscape is flat and two-dimensional. Its deceptive flatness obscures microelevations and microterrains that add diversity to the ecosystem. The horizontal nature of the land shrouds magnificent habitats, wildness, and cultural riches. Access to a number of destinations requires travel on unpaved roads and long stretches of unmarked waters. In the warm months, visitors who leave the sanctuary of their air-conditioned vehicles may find it an inhospitable world of biting insects. The Santee Delta is not a shrine to history like Charleston, replete with horse-drawn carriage tours and a living streetscape museum experience; its rich stories and treasures are mostly unspoken and unseen.

• CHAPTER •

THE PREHISTORIC DELTA

The great river's tributaries, swelled by the enormous watershed, carried its sediment-laden waters toward the ocean. Throughout the coastal plain, the Santee River rose during high waters, overflowing the banks and spreading out through the forest. It was not just any forest, but one adapted to frequent flooding. This floodplain swamp is an incredibly dynamic environment, made up of several forest communities. The flora trapped and cycled nutrients during these floods, which acted as side trips for the water and sediments from their initial destination of the Atlantic Ocean. No plant was better adapted for these conditions than the cypress tree.[1]

Bald cypress *Taxodium distichum* has dominated swamps all along the Santee. Evidence in the form of old cypress stumps is scattered throughout the twenty-first century Santee Delta. This tree species, kin to West Coast redwoods, has a number of special characteristics. Some specimens have grown over 1,000 years old, and stand over 120 feet tall. Above the natural swelling of the buttressed bases, diameters can measure up to ten feet. One unique adaptation to flooding and rooting in muddy soils is the presence of vertical structures—cypress knees—growing apart from the tree base. Despite the unstable nature of soils in cypress swamps, cypress trees are rarely uprooted by wind.[2]

Swamp forest in Audubon's Beidler Forest Sanctuary.

This tree species caught the attention and wonder of several eighteenth-century naturalists. William Bartram's observations of cypress trees are an excellent example of his admiration for the tree, and nature in general:

> *The* Cupressus disticha *stands in the first order of North American trees. Its majestic stature is surprising, and on approaching them, we are struck with a kind of awe, at beholding the stateliness of the trunk, lifting its cumbrous top towards the skies, and casting a wide shade upon the ground, as a dark intervening cloud, which for a time, precludes the rays of the sun. The delicacy of its colour,*

and texture of its leaves, exceed everything in vegetation... The large ones are hollow, and serve very well for beehives; a small space of the tree itself is hollow, nearly as high as the buttresses already mentioned. From this place the tree, as it were, takes another beginning, forming a grand strait column eighty or ninety feet high, when it divides every way around into an extensive flat horizontal top, like an umbrella, where eagles have their secure nests, and cranes and storks their temporary resting places; and what adds to the magnificence of their appearance, is the streamers of long moss that hang from the lofty limbs and float in the winds. This is their majestic appearance, when standing alone, in large rice plantations, or thinly planted on the banks of great rivers.[3]

Before Bartram, John Lawson in his travels considered them "the largest for Height and Thickness, that we have in this Part of the World; some of them holding thirty-six Foot in Circumference." Cypresses are distinctive trees, and each cypress swamp has a unique identity.[4]

The prehistoric Santee Delta's swamp forest was most likely a mix of bald cypress and tupelo gum trees. Though there are no extant portions of that original forest, a younger version is reappearing in the Wambaw Creek Wilderness Area. Paddling along the Wambaw, one intermittently encounters a grizzled and gnarled ancient, perhaps left by timber cutters due to its defects. That Wambaw cypress-gum successional forest continues to regenerate.

To imagine the Delta's virgin floodplain forest, we can use the example of the current 1,800-acre tract of original growth forest at Audubon's Francis Beidler Forest in Harleyville, and a survey of its vascular flora published in 1981 by then Citadel botany professor Richard Porcher. Two floodplain forest communities that composed the prehistoric Delta are well represented at Beidler: swamp forest and hardwood bottomland forest. The mature swamp forest at Beidler Forest is dominated by two tree species: bald cypress and tupelo gum. The cypress trees form the canopy up to 120 feet in height; the tupelo gums form a subcanopy eighty feet high. The Beidler cypresses measure up to five to six feet in diameter and up to seven hundred to eight hundred years in age. In the deepest water and the lowest elevations exist almost pure stands of cypress and tupelo. In even small elevation rises in the swamp forest, other distinctive forest communities exist. The hydromorphic adaptations of the cypresses and tupelos—buttresses and knees—provide the substrate for another group of trees to grow. Water ash trees form a lower subcanopy. Two other hydric species mixed in are honey locust and water elm. Four other species common in hardwood bottom forests and growing on fallen logs, knees, and buttresses in the swamp forest are swamp laurel oak, red maple, sweet gum, and American elm.[5]

As the floodplain elevation increases at Beidler, the hardwood bottom forest community dominates. This forest ecosystem would have also occurred in the Santee Delta as isolated "islands" of higher elevation relative to the surrounding swamp forest. At Beidler, the predominating trees in the hardwood bottom forest are oaks forming the canopy with some occasional cypress. The canopy trees are water hickory, overcup oak, water oak, willow oak, and swamp laurel oak, along with red maple, sweetgum, American elm, water ash, tupelo gum, sour gum, and Southern hackberry. At higher elevations, dwarf palmetto densely populated the limited shrub layer.[6]

What might a Native American have experienced paddling through the Delta's virgin floodplain forest before the impact from the influx of immigrants? John Lawson's travels through the Santee Delta in 1701 provide a window into the challenges of navigating a flooded forest. Scipio, the Sewee Indian, had piloted the group across the river. Their next destination was the house of "Mons. Galliar's, jun'," and even their Sewee guide lost his bearings due to the forest "having receiv'd so strange a Metamorphosis." There was not room in the canoe for all, and it was decided to send Scipio with half the group. Lawson and the other stranded group members anxiously waited on a dry spot for six hours before the return of their guide. After paddling several miles through the flooded forest in a canoe at times half-filled with water, they arrived safely at their destination. As they later proceeded from Barthélémy Gaillard's on foot, they made a ten-mile detour to bypass the flooded swamp.[7]

The Pee Dee River to the north combining with the Santee has created the largest deltaic bulge on the East Coast. One hypothesis suggests that the Pee Dee and Santee were joined in "the Greater Santee River" in the not distant geological past. Adjacent to the Delta are a number of parallel former beach ridges from the late Pleistocene epoch. These ridges were cut through during the late Wisconsin drop in sea level and the formation of the Santee River valley. The geologists Miles Hayes and Jacqueline Michel divide the Delta into three components: upper delta plain, lower delta plain, and delta front. The inland limit of the upper delta plain is approximately where the current "head of the tides" exists, along with the serpentine main channel of the Santee. The Santee divides into two channels, the North and South Santee Rivers, in this upper delta plain. Historically the main flow switched between the two systems, though currently the North Santee has that distinction.[8]

We must back up from the relatively recent to distant geological time to understand the dynamics of the Santee River and Santee Delta. It is a complex story spanning hundreds of millions of years and challenging a nongeologist's powers of comprehension. Plunging back into deep time and into the world of plate tectonics, the various continental plates moving across the earth's surface alternately fused into supercontinents and then divided. The collision of these plates caused mountain-building events on our continent known by geologists as orogenies, and three figured in the Carolina mountains: the Grenville, the Taconic, and the Alleghenian. The Appalachians were thrust up to Andean and even Himalayan heights during this mountain building. Over millions of years the process of erosion by weather and water has worn these mountains down to their current height. The extensive Santee River system has contributed to this erosion, carrying sediments downstream to the coastal plain and Atlantic Ocean.[9]

Prior to 1942, the Santee River was the fourth largest river on the East Coast in terms of discharge, having an annual mean discharge of $525 m^3 s^{-1}$ (cubic meters per second). Periodic floods known as freshets were significant events beyond the normal cyclic floods. The huge watershed of the Santee drains the three physiographic provinces of the Carolinas: the Blue Ridge, the Piedmont, and the Coastal Plain. The sediment load of these waters would contribute to the physical development of the Delta, the nature of the bays behind the barrier islands, and the navigability of the two inlets.[10]

It would be a mistake to imagine the Santee Delta as an untouched wilderness prior to contact by Europeans. There is evidence that Native Americans changed the natural landscape. In John Lawson's journey through the Delta in 1701, he observed Sewee Indians setting fires to the "Cane swamps," located along riverbanks. The Sewees were using fire "which drives out the Game, then taking their particular Stands, kill great Quantities of both Bear, Deer, Turkies, and what wild Creatures the Parts afford." Indians would also have harvested suitable trees for dugout canoes.[11]

Other exploring naturalists in the eighteenth century described the canebrake ecosystem in the Southeast, a monoculture of this cane, the only bamboo native to North America. Mark Catesby observed these canebrakes in his travels in the 1720s, describing the vast thickets as twenty to thirty feet high and quite dense. Later in the century, William Bartram described the "most extensive Cane-break that is to be seen on the face of the whole earth." Lawson's account documents the existence of large canebrakes in the Santee Delta and the Sewees' use of fire in driving game. Periodic burning of the quite flammable canebrakes by Indians maintained the canebrake ecosystem.[12]

These canes were an important botanical resource of Native Americans in the Southeast. While they occurred in various forest types, the largest canebrakes existed along the natural levees of the alluvial floodplains of the brownwater rivers. Indians used cane for many purposes. It was a very useful building material for dwellings and structures. Cane provided raw material for arrow shafts, knives, blowguns, and shields. Specialized arrows and spears for fishing were fashioned from canes, and cane weirs were built to trap fish. Canebrakes were a valued area for hunting since they provided habitat for a number of wildlife species. The capacity of cane for burning contributed to the firing of canebrakes to drive wildlife in hunts. Domestic uses included the building of furniture, mats for seating, and basketry. The great canebrakes of the Southeast and specifically those of the Santee Delta gradually disappeared after European colonization.[13]

I set out in November 2011 from the North Santee's Pole Yard to visit a little-known archaeological site tagged 38GE46. My only other trip from this landing was on a long sail tracing the Inland Passage[14] from here to Charleston Harbor in September 2007, a voyage successfully facilitated by a steady northeast wind of fifteen to twenty knots and ideal tides. I again used my Sunfish class sailboat *Kingfisher*, and the southwest winds appeared favorable. In hindsight, it was the wrong tide, the wrong boat, and the wrong day to attempt this trip to this archaeological site, but I was determined.

It was a struggle making progress at the beginning of the sail due to a light wind, the wind-blockage of trees on the river's bank, and an adverse tide. The initial voyage impediments dissipated with a rising wind. Wildlife encounters included a sizable alligator on the bank and an eagle at the entrance to Minim Creek. The wind continued to rise, and prior to entering the Intracoastal Waterway, I pulled on a rain gear top and lifejacket to block the cold November spray. I bore off onto a run in the waterway and noted the increased wind and chop, the conditions I would face on the return sail. I was fortunate to not capsize when I lost control and spun 180 degrees head-to-wind.

Searching for 38GE46's location using a hand-drawn map, I zeroed in on a stand of red cedars as the likely spot and came in under sail into the marsh grass. I left the sail up and secured *Kingfisher* to a small cedar. One of my first steps on this beach was right next to a potsherd exposing the spot's tantalizing prehistory. The human occupation of the site dates back to the early Woodland period, with ceramic artifacts categorized as Thom's Creek/Refuge assembly (to 1440 BC). It was a seasonal campsite used in spring and summer for subsistence on estuarine fish, especially sturgeon and gar, and in fall for oyster harvest. The seasonal occupants had deposited a sizable shell midden over five feet thick in places during the early Deptford occupation, around 600–250 BC. Archaeologists had found Deptford Check Stamped pottery in this midden along with many oyster shells, and remains from fish and mammals. This site had been a permanent seasonal camp for a few families, and the use of the camp dropped off in the post-Deptford period. This decline was the result of a gradual sea level rise from the early Woodland period to the present. Local oyster beds disappeared, and the movement of estuarine fishes changed.[15]

Brockington and Associates, a cultural resources firm, studied this prehistoric site in 1989. They initiated the work due to the erosion caused by the inland waterway action exacerbated by boat wakes. In the wrack of tidal debris, I found a fine potsherd from a rim, rounded and punctate. A large sloop heading south slowly motored by in the waterway, and the skipper seemed concerned about my condition. His concern was understandable due to the location's remoteness and my craft pulled up in the marsh grass, but I reassured him with a thumbs-up. After my brief visit to this disappearing archaeological site, I got underway for the return sail. The sailing was challenging, initially due to the wind and chop in the ICW, and later by the dropping of the wind and outgoing tide. For the last mile, intermittent use of the paddle gave way to sole paddling for propulsion to reach the Pole Yard Landing. At 4 p.m., I was the last landing user of the day.

Trip to rapidly eroding site 38GE46 along Intracoastal Waterway in 2011.

The place name of the 38GE46 site has disappeared, along with much of the indigenous history of the Santee Delta. People continue to find prehistoric artifacts in the Delta, and surely future archaeological investigations will identify other important sites. What remains is an assortment of place names dotting the area that provide a connection to these peoples: Santee, the primary river running through the Delta, and the name of a people once living further upriver; a number of creeks flowing into the Santee: Wambaw, Washaw, Wahaw, Echaw, Mechaw, and Washasha; a plantation named for the place name, Watahan. Upstream, a few tributaries of the Santee retain their indigenous names, and Native American tribes shared these names: Congaree, Wateree, and Catawba.

Contact by indigenous South Carolinas with Europeans came well before the *Carolina* arrived with English colonists in 1670. The Spanish had a presence in the Southeast predating the English incursion. Expeditions by Hernando de Soto in 1541 and by Juan Pardo in 1566 and 1567-68 had traveled through South Carolina and interacted with Native Americans. The Spanish had also established a fort and settlement at Santa Elena on Parris Island in Beaufort County. From a base in St. Augustine, and responding to rumors of an English colony along the coast, Captain Francisco Fernandez de Ecija and his forces set off to search out the English in 1605. When their ship entered the Santee River, the Spanish called it the "River Jordan." Due to the strong current, efforts to sail up the river were futile. Ecija obtained intelligence from local Indians, not just about the English but also the Indians of the interior. He learned that those interior people brought skins, copper, and other metals to the coast to trade for fish, salt, and shellfish. The source of the copper was a town called Xoada near the mountains; both de Soto and Pardo earlier visited this place.[16]

The Santee provided passage through the Delta for Indians for thousands of years before Europeans entered the picture. Yet predating man's occupation, beneath the river's surface fish had passed through on their great migration journeys. A number of anadromous fishes, including the Atlantic sturgeon, the American shad, and the blueback herring, traveled from the Atlantic Ocean far up the Santee to spawn, as these fish species have done on other rivers along the East Coast. The mature sturgeon sought a hard clay, rubble, or gravel bottom in well-oxygenated water to spawn. The juvenile sturgeon would spend their first years in the river's estuary before migrating to the ocean. Mature Atlantic sturgeons have grown to a length over ten feet, with females the larger fish. The American shad ascends the river to freshwater, and further than other members of the *Alosa* family. Historical accounts of shad fisheries in the early nineteenth century exist for locations on the Congaree River above the confluence with the Wateree.[17]

Migrating above the waters and perpendicular to the course of fish have been innumerable waterfowl along the Atlantic Flyway. They navigated south before winter and returned to their summer breeding grounds in the spring. The waterfowl flew into the Delta before the presence of indigenous peoples. These birds would have included the dabbling duck family: mallards, American wigeons, northern shovelers, teals, wood ducks, black ducks, gadwalls, whistling ducks; the diving duck family: canvasbacks, redheads, ringnecks, scaups, buffleheads, mergansers, scoters; and swans and geese.

Throughout the Santee Delta, the miraculous migratory journeys of wildlife have carried on persistently: shad swimming in from the Atlantic to find their entrance to the Santee and spawning grounds upstream, waterfowl flying in to bays and ponds to feed, and loggerhead turtles coming back to natal beaches to nest.

The merging of the fresh and salt waters provided bountiful conditions in the estuary, attracting the seasonal residence of Native Americans. The brackish waters were the foundation for a unique ecosystem considered to be one of the most productive in the world and supporting diverse communities of plant and animal species. The Santee Delta's estuary is partially enclosed by three barrier islands: South, Cedar, and Murphy Islands. The estuarine habitats allowed animals to forage for food, to nest, and to breed. The marshes encompassed a range of habitats, formed on a gradient created through varying salinity: freshwater, brackish, and salt. In terms of water circulation, the Delta was highly stratified, creating a salt wedge due to the massive flow of freshwater draining the Santee basin. The barrier islands of the Delta had the main features of other South Carolina barriers: sand beaches and dunes, maritime forests, and salt marshes on the islands' backside.

The unique nature of the Santee River and Santee Delta along the South Carolina coast would shape the Delta's future. The Santee Delta's lack of a deep-water harbor and navigable access to the protected waters, unlike the natural conditions of Charleston Harbor, Port Royal Sound, and Georgetown, would rule out any viable port considerations. The presence of the salt wedge led to the transformation of the Delta into a lucrative center of the Rice Kingdom.

The estuary and its wetlands were rich habitats for migratory waterfowl, which would spur a remarkable chain of events leading to conservation efforts in the Santee Delta.

· CHAPTER ·

THE COMMAND OF WATER

One of the renowned eighteenth-century naturalists who traveled through the Lowcountry was John Bartram. Bartram — father of the equally famous William Bartram — was a humble farmer and plant collector, yet his garden along the Schuylkill River outside Philadelphia became famous. He was a friend to founding fathers, and a skilled self-taught botanist. On his travels through the Southeast in the 1760s, Bartram observed a farm in a diary entry, "thair best rice ground is where they have ye command of water in ye dryest season."[1]

In the earliest days of rice culture in South Carolina, irrigation occurred only by the good fortune of rain. This process was providence rice culture, water provided by the skies. Improved agricultural practice required the "command of water." An early effort at harnessing water in rice cultivation led to reservoir culture, where planters used impounded waters to flood rice fields. Peoples throughout the world had used the technique for hundreds of years, including in West Africa. The use of reservoirs to flood rice fields was most common in inland swamps, such as the Wambaw Swamp. Water use irrigated plants and controlled weeds in rice fields. Drought dried up reservoirs and jeopardized inland rice culture.

Sometime in the eighteenth century, planters moved rice culture to the banks of rivers. The diurnal pulse of the tides provided a reliable source for water irrigation of rice. The estuary of the Santee Delta had distinct hydrological characteristics advantageous to rice culture. The strong freshwater flow coming down the Santee created a sharp stratification between the fresh and salt water; the incoming saltwater tide pushed the freshwater back into the Delta, and a saltwater wedge drove beneath the fresh. Since the Santee River encompassed a vast floodplain basin, the great flow of freshwater allowed rice culture within miles of the ocean, even on easternmost Murphy, Cedar, and South Islands. The increased productivity of tidal irrigation versus reservoir irrigation was significant: 1,200 to 1,500 pounds per acre compared to 600 to 1,000 pounds per acre.[2]

The process of riverine rice field development began with a survey setting off the boundaries of the field from river's edge to upland. Enslaved laborers cleared vegetation from the location of the permanent bank, and raised a temporary bank on the riverside of the permanent bank's placement. A shallow ditch dug in the location of the permanent bank provided the soil for the temporary bank, and the removal of tree stumps from that ditch ensured no voids from decaying tree remnants would jeopardize the final dike. With the area protected from tides for the permanent construction, workers dug the main ditch, eight feet wide and five feet deep. They used some of the soil to fill the temporary ditch, and more to create the permanent bank, twelve feet wide and two feet higher than spring tides.[3]

Land clearing came next, a monumental undertaking due to the mature swamp forest. In the late eighteenth century, William Bartram described the method used by planters to fell the huge cypress trees. Enslaved laborers raised staging above the buttresses of the cypress, and eight to ten men would work at that level with axes to fell the massive tree. In the nineteenth century, two accomplished rice planters recorded their process for land clearing. David Doar, one of the last large scale rice planters in the Santee Delta, described cutting and burning small trees and underbrush, and grubbing out the stumps. Men girdled large trees and later cut them down at ground level, the timber used for other plantation purposes. The largest stumps were left in the field. J. Motte Alston on the Waccamaw River described in detail the cutting down of the cane, the small growth, and then timber of all sizes, cut to within two feet of the ground. Workers cut the tree trunks into ten-foot lengths, and after drying for months burned the debris piles.[4]

After clearing, the laborers subdivided the large embanked area into twenty-acre units, each field having its own banks and ditches, and leveled the land of each field for the controlled flooding to evenly cover the soil. Reflecting on the totality of rice field development, J. Motte Alston observed, "The axes are ringing

Felling a tree in the Santee Swamp - south of Jordan's Cross Roads, Clarendon County, S.C. Though this photo was taken in 1940 during the clearing for Lake Marion, the earlier cutting down of swamp forest in the Santee Delta used similar tools and methods for felling trees.

through the dense swamp and glimpses of light is seen, as one by one the tall trees come crashing to the earth to make way, in time for waving fields of green and gold. The work is slow and arduous, week by week, month by month, year by year." The development of the rice fields transformed the landscape throughout the Santee Delta. Ten thousand acres of swamp forest fell before the axes.[5]

For this enterprise, planters marshaled the labor of a large enslaved workforce. The requirements of rice culture development and the need for slave labor stimulated the increased importation of enslaved West Africans to the Lowcountry. The work was brutal, dangerous, and often fatal for the enslaved laborers. It is difficult to comprehend the extent of the exertion required to accomplish the tasks described above. I have dropped small trees with an ax, and grubbed out small stumps with hand tools. Yet from my efforts, I only have a meager sense of the historic ordeal. Add into the rice swamps the heat and humidity of a Lowcountry summer day, the presence of biting insects filling the air and water moccasins underfoot, and the lack of suitable clothing and footwear, and you may distantly imagine the deadly difficulties of the labor. Alston's observation that "the work is slow and arduous, week by week, etc," if considered over the long term by the enslaved, could easily have resulted in despair. How did people cope with this enslavement and enforced labor? How did they survive the deadly ordeal of transportation across the horrible Middle Passage? According to some historians, the foundation of African religious and cultural beliefs enabled the survival and transition to the rice plantations for many Africans.[6]

The sluice allowing for precise flooding was a device called the rice trunk. The process of building and installing these hydrological machines required significant skill and effort. For the installation, workers removed a section of the bank and prepared the bottom of this gap to receive the trunk. At slack tide, the laborers placed the trunk in the hole, packed soil around the device up to the bank's top, and lastly hung the gates of the trunk. With a flawed installation, the tide's pressure could cause the trunk to "blow." Each twenty-acre field had its own trunk, and the water level flooded or drained independently of other fields. Quarter drains subdivided each field and drained into the main ditch.[7]

For the best practice of rice cultivation, finely crafted rice trunks were a necessity, and a valued artisan on the plantation was the trunk builder. Jane Wineglass was the fifteenth child of Sambo and Eve Green, and stated her father was a carpenter who had a reputation for doing "neat work," including building trunks. Sambo Green worked at times for Archibald Rutledge of Hampton Plantation, and Rutledge described Green and his craft. "Old Sambo Green is the only Negro I know who can make one of these wooden floodgates which, by a kind of hydraulic magic, harness the tides. . . . Sambo Green is old, small, mild-mannered, peering. He is well over seventy, and he walks stoopingly and unsteadily. To me he illustrates the fine principle that skill, intelligence, and gentleness are often of far more effect than brute strength. I have many Negroes that could tie Sambo up with one hand, but not one of them can make a trunk. Nature endowed him with this certain, if slight, wizardry, and long experience has made him a master in his field."[8]

Starting with a pile of three-inch-thick planks, Green set to work with only a few tools: an auger, a saw, a hatchet, and an old plane. Rutledge understood Green's real tools were "his understanding heart, his seeing eye of his sensitive, intelligent hands." Green walked the four miles each way from his home at Collins Creek to Hampton daily. He built and installed the trunk with such

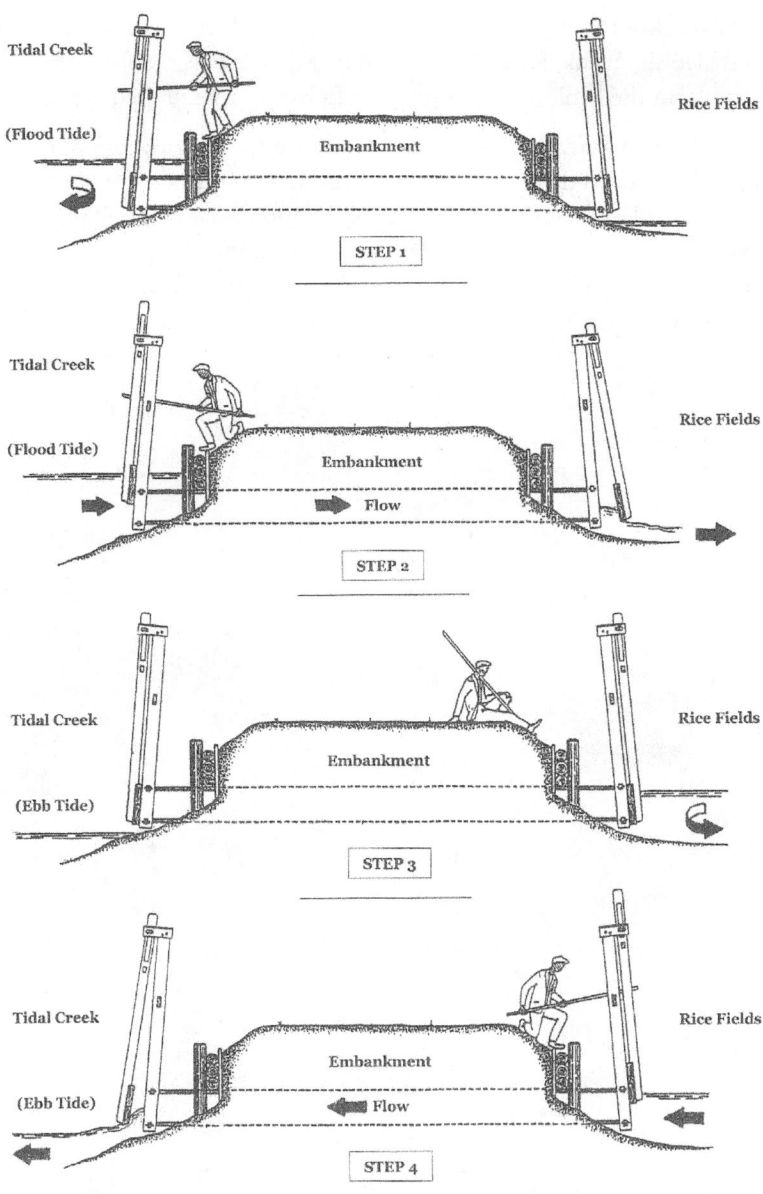

Operation of a tide trunk. Illustrations by William Robert Judd.

precision that it could flow water onto a field within a fraction of an inch. Twenty days after the start of construction, Green with the help of twenty other men installed the trunk. Rutledge asserted that this device, similar to the other older trunks in the banks of Hampton, would last over a hundred years.⁹

The command of water by tide trunks allowed for the flow culture of rice. The process included three main parts: the sprout flow, the stretch flow, and the harvest flow. Colonel Joshua J. Ward, one of the most accomplished planters in the Lowcountry on the Waccamaw River, described the best practices in rice culture and the use of tidal irrigation in 1850 as reported to the Winyah Agricultural Society.

Rice trunk and impoundment in the Santee Delta.

It is scarcely necessary to observe that the Land should be in good order; That is, that the Banks and Trunks, should be in such condition as to keep the Water Within or Without the fields, as circumstance may render necessary; The Drains ought to be 37-1/2 to 50 feet apart, & at least 3 feet deep and eighteen inches wide. It is evidently important that every part of the fields, should be as nearly as possible, in same condition as regards hoeing &c when the Water is put on; otherwise, from the different state of the Plant one portion would require different Treatment from another, which, of course, is impossible. During the Winter, the land ought to be well turned either by plow or hoe. As planting time approaches, the land should be well marked and laid off in bold trenches, with a 4 inch 'Trenching Hoe', 13 inches from centre to centre; the seed is to be carefully sowed at a rate of from 2 1/2 to 3 bushels, the Acre, according to Order land may be in. The greater quantity to be used when it is not in best State of preparation. There are different opinions on the subject of covering the seed; on low gummy lands, the open planting is best, but when soil is well prepared a careful covering is to be preferred. The Sprout Water is then put on, and Remains until grain 'pips', which will take place according to the Weather from 3 to 6 days; The water is then taken off & land kept as dry as possible, until you can see the rice the whole length of the Row across the bed, coming out in fine Sprigs called the 'Needle State,' the Point flow is then put on and retained from 3 to 6 days, or as long as it can be kept on without Weakening the plant so much as to cause it to fall when Water is taken from it. This is especially important, as the grass being young is more effectually destroyed than at any later Stage of the crop. As soon as rice is Strong enough, a light hoeing should be given it with a six inch Rice Hoe. About 12 days after this, it should be well stirred with 6 inch hoe again, and allow two or three days for Sun to kill grass, disturbed by hoe. The Long water is then put on, and the Rice to be overtopped for three or four days, the trash which will float must be carefully raked on the Banks. By this Deep flow, not only the trash is removed but the insects with which the Rice is infested are for the time completely Destroyed. The water is then gradually Slackened, to about Six inches Deep on general level. A notch must be made on Trunk or elsewhere, and water kept, by this, as near the Same level as can be, for from twelve to twenty three days, according to the quality of land, the heavy land requiring the longest Water. The Water, however, should not be taken off on Fifteenth day, as from State of plant at that time, it is apt to 'Fox' or turn Bad.

The water is then to be gradually slackened off to prevent the rice from falling in in low parts of field, it being weak from greater depth of Water; and this points out the great importance of bringing the surface of every rice field, as nearly as may be to a level, as in lower spots rice is often materially injured, & in high places grass is not Destroyed.

> When Water is off surface, the trunks are to be thrown open, & the land again kept as dry as possible. During this flow, or Rather about the time of Slacking off as what grass may have escaped the hoe will have grown Rapidly, it is advisable to turn the 'Hands' in & pick it out. As soon as land is sufficiently Dry, it is to be Dug as deep as practicable with 4 inch rice hoe, to enable the Roots of the plant to spread with greater facility. In about 22 days after 'Long Water' the fourth and last hoeing should be given with a 4 inch hoe, and should be very light, merely to level clods left from the digging and to destroy young grass, particular care being taken not to injure or disturb the roots of the plant. A day or two after this hoeing, the 'Layby' water should be put on, about same Depth, or perhaps a little Deeper than the Long water notch; lower or higher according to growth of Rice. Care should be taken that when rice begins to Round (or ear formed) that the water should not get over the 'fork'. It is to be noticed, that as soon as the Weaker portions of the Rice gains sufficient strength, the Water should be changed at Stated times, which should be regularly attended to until crop is ready for the Hook.[10]

The world of rice culture had its own lexicon of water as described in Ward's account: the "sprout water" used to germinate the seeds, the "point flow" used to hold the tender plants up, and the "long water" used to float off the trash, kill insects, and irrigate the rice plants for the longest duration in the growing season. Some planters combined both the point flow and long water without a pause into the "stretch flow." And finally, the "layby water" or "harvest flow" used as the final irrigation to support the weight of the grain ripening before harvest. Ward's description spells out the exacting nature of the timing of the irrigation and the periodic hoeing in producing the best crop. The trunk minder, a specialized worker in the labor force, controlled the precise level of water moving into and out of the rice fields in rhythm with the irrigation needs and the tides. The job of trunk minder has carried over into the present. William Garrett grew up on Blake's Plantation, worked as a guide at the Santee Gun Club, and later as an employee of Santee Coastal Reserve. He recalled his father serving in the role of trunk minder on Blake's Plantation.[11]

These hydraulic devices only worked with the massive infrastructure of the built banks, their immensity compared to the great pyramids. Phil Wilkinson grew up in the Santee Delta, and after obtaining a graduate degree and employment with the state wildlife department, Tom Yawkey hired him for wildlife management at his South Island Plantation. Wilkinson went further in the pyramid analogy to suggest that the extent of labor represented more than one pyramid. He noted that just on South Island, there were thirty miles of dikes, counting only the current banks around managed impoundments. After he began work at Santee

Rice harvest at Annandale Plantation, 1921.

Coastal Reserve, Bill Mace expressed his incredulity to his Black crew about the work required to build the forty miles of banks. Johnny Garrett, a former Santee Gun Club guide, and brother of William, stated to Mace that perhaps three to four hundred men built that dike "passing the mud, digging the canal, passing the mud, stacking it, doing it all by hand." In 1765, on a journey through the Southeast, John Bartram observed a group of 130 enslaved workers digging a ditch near the Edisto River. In many stages of the command of water, enslaved Africans achieved the remarkable outcomes. As observed by Phil Wilkinson, workers now use modern heavy equipment to make bank improvements. These modern developments do not diminish the monumental works accomplished by the enslaved labor force.[12]

These banks needed maintenance, and planters found the slack period in winter after cultivation a time to direct their enslaved laborers to work on the dikes. The enslaved found it one of the more odious tasks – often accomplished in cold, wet, and unpleasant conditions. During Reconstruction and in the transition to the labor of free African Americans, rice laborers began to refuse this "mud work."[13]

Some have assumed that dike construction and maintenance was unskilled, but Archibald Rutledge cited the opposite with the example of Alex, a local ferryman, who was an expert in building banks. Rutledge's description of Alex at work is instructive.

> *Standing on the quaking morass of a rice field, Alex, with three deft strokes of his spade, cuts loose from its melancholy mooring a block of mud about three times as big as a brick. With matchless co-ordination of muscle and of eye, he heaves the block of mud fifteen or twenty feet to the top of the bank that is being raised.*
>
> *The mud must not merely be thrown but must be thrown upward, and often Alex cannot see what might be termed his target. But he makes the block fall flat; it falls exactly in place, close to the one that preceded it. And almost before it has settled securely, here comes another. This heavy mud is laid, from a distance, just as bricks are laid. It is like some magic remote-control building of a wall, with the bricklayer twenty feet away.*
>
> *Alex can keep this up by the hour, with a tireless rhythm that is profoundly discouraging to all his would-be imitators.*[14]

A belief has existed that slave labor was synonymous with unskilled labor. Scholarship has provided evidence for the familiarity and skill of West Africans with rice culture. While not every African had this background, a sizable group of the enslaved had more experience than the European settlers. Many African women had skills in both rice culture and processing. In South Carolina, between 1750 and 1775, planters preferred importing people from the area of West Africa associated with rice cultivation.[15]

The labor system utilized generally on rice plantations was the task system, organized in sharp contrast to the use of gang labor on cotton plantations. In breaking up ground, hoeing one quarter of an acre was a common task. The overseer assigned each enslaved person a description relative to their age and physical capacity for work: full-task hands, three quarter-task hands, etc., and calculated what could be accomplished in nine hours with the laborer working steadily. The orderly grid of the rice field was conducive for assignment of work in the task system. The system created a strong incentive: after the completion of the task, the individual was free to see to personal needs, such as tending a personal garden or fishing. Both reservoir culture and tidal culture used the task system.¹⁶

Larger ditches formed canals in the rice fields that would connect to rice fields and smaller ditches located further from the rivers. These manmade waterways were especially important for large plantations where many rice fields were not adjacent to the river. The size of these canals permitted a distinctive Lowcountry watercraft, the rice flat, to navigate these waters and move from river to rice field. Floodgates, built at the junction between the canal and river, allowed the flats to enter and exit the rice fields and navigate the rivers. These canals facilitated the flooding and draining of the back rice fields. During a 2007 duck hunt on Murphy Island that I observed, Bill Mace used a johnboat to navigate these larger canals at speed in depositing the hunters at their assigned blinds.¹⁷

Rice flats were one form of watercraft of the rice plantation. These barges or flats were easy to construct, shallow draft, and utilitarian. Their most important cargo was rice during the harvest, though they also transported workers, tools and materials, mud for bank repairs, pile drivers, and even new trunks. Typical rice flats were thirty-five to fifty feet long, eleven to fourteen feet wide, and a depth of two to three feet, with the ability to carry two to three tons. Watermen propelled the flats by oars, and poles in the rice fields. The larger flats also transported goods to market.¹⁸

The rice flat reflected the design of ferry craft. Transportation in the Lowcountry, particularly in moving cargoes, depended on the myriad waterways and various classes of watercraft. Travelers often found roads impassable in wet weather. Movement of people and goods by land was most dependent on a viable ferry system for crossing rivers. The Santee Delta presented a significant barrier for transit: two deep rivers (the North and South Santee Rivers), and a wide delta of marsh.

In 1737 William Mazyck purchased Romney, a five-hundred-acre plantation on the south side of the South Santee River, and acquired the rights to a ferry site operated by Joseph Spencer and earlier by Ralph Jermain. For travelers heading north, this ferry began their Delta crossing. The ferry could carry horses as well as carriages. Prior to the building of a causeway over the Delta marshes on what came to be known as Lynch's Island, the ferry utilized Push and Go Creek, spelling out the propulsion of the ferry by men poling their ferryboat. In 1737

Moving the rice trunk, Kinloch Plantation. These men are poling a rice flat that is carrying a rice trunk, most likely to the site of its installation.

William Buchanan gained the rights of operating the ferry over the North Santee River. Ferry owners received tolls for the service. An act of 1737 required both Mazyck and Buchanan to keep a canoe and a ferryboat with two or more men prepared to take care of travelers. The provincial government specified one white man to be posted on each ferry to check the identities of travelers, particularly screening for runaway slaves. While the ferries had the primary function of transporting travelers over the rivers, they also restricted the mobility of the enslaved.[19]

The ferry crossing of the Santee Delta had its challenges. In 1789 the French naturalist André Michaux was returning by horseback to his Charleston-area plantation after visiting Philadelphia and his friend William Bartram. High winds detained him and his son François André for two nights before the ferry operator transported them and their horses across the Delta. I can only imagine the difficult summer conditions along the North Santee River, though perhaps the high winds relieved the plague of biting insects.[20]

Ferries carried travelers over the North and South Santee until bridges spanned these rivers in the twentieth century. In 1792, one carriage with a famous entourage headed south. George Washington on a southern tour during his presidency traveled from Georgetown to Charleston and planned a stop at Hampton Plantation. The carriage passengers included some notable Lowcountry residents: William Moultrie, Thomas Pinckney, William Washington, and John Rutledge Jr. Harriott Pinckney Horry and her mother, Eliza Lucas Pinckney, hosted their visit at Hampton.[21]

While designated ferries were the regulated means of crossing the Santee, anyone with a boat could do the same. In the Revolutionary War, the Santee was a barrier for the British traveling from Charleston (during the British occupation) to Camden. General Francis Marion directed one of his officers, Peter Horry, to "take command of such men as will be collected from Capts. Bonneau, Mitchell and Benson's companies and proceed to Santee from the lower ferry [Lynch's or Mazyck's Ferry] to Lenud's and destroy all boats and canoes on river and post guards so as to prevent persons crossing to us from Charleston on either side of river." Horry wrote later about destroying not just the flats at the ferries, but every skiff and canoe found. This action did not sit well with the planters owning these craft. "Among the fleet of boats and flats that perished by our firebrands or hatchets, there were two that belonged to my excellent old uncle, Colonel E(lias) Horry. The old Gentleman could hardly believe his Negroes, when they told him that we were destroying his boats."[22]

One of the coveted jobs among the enslaved on Lowcountry rice plantations was boatman. This position took the worker out of field labor and afforded him the relative freedom to travel between country plantation and town. Planters recognized the boat handling skills of many Africans, and gave the most skilled boatmen the designation of "patroon," or skipper of the craft, which included dugouts, flats, and even small schooners. This ability to travel the Lowcountry waterways created the opportunity for unsanctioned enterprise. Henry Laurens complained to Abraham Schad, the overseer at his Wambaw Plantation, about his enslaved boatman Amos for "a great inclination to turn rum merchant."[23]

Knowledge of the waterways and access to watercraft provided the opportunity for enslaved people to seek full freedom by running away from their plantation servitude. A *City Gazette* advertisement in 1795 gave the story of one such Santee boatman.

> ## Thirty Dollars Reward
>
> LEFT Santee a few days ago, a NEGRO FELLOW named JACK, belonging to the estate of Daniel Horry, esq.; he is a good boatman and pilot, very artful and sensible, and may call himself a free man, having a pass he received from the British during the war; he went off with a canoe with a sail, and is supposed will attempt to go to St. Augustine, or otherwise to ship himself in some vessel for the West-Indies. JACK is very well known in Charleston, and has a sister at Mr. Sims White's. Whoever will apprehend the said fellow and deliver him to Mr. Snyder, at Santee, or to the master of the work-house, in Charleston, shall be entitled to the above reward. All masters of vessels and others are cautioned not to harbor or carry him off the state, as they will be prosecuted to the utmost rigor of the law.
>
> November 12. [24]

The Daniel Horry mentioned in the *Gazette* was Daniel Huger Horry, the husband of Harriot Pinckney Horry. She had taken over management of their plantations on the South Santee including Hampton during the Revolution when her husband traveled to England, and later after his death. Though the *Gazette* advertisement referred to Jack as belonging to the estate of Daniel Horry, enslaved people of the Horry family were later known as "Mrs. Horry's Negroes."

About thirty years before, two other enslaved Africans had made a brief run for freedom, though no details of their escape and later capture from Henry Laurens and John Coming Ball's Wambaw Plantation remain. These two men were part of a larger group of twenty-seven individuals purchased by Laurens from the firm Brailsford and Chapman. They experienced the Middle Passage across the Atlantic to Charleston from West Africa and then to Wambaw Plantation. Laurens shipped the two runaways, Aaron and James, via schooner for sale in Georgetown, after their capture.[25]

The canoe that Jack used on his run for freedom was a ubiquitous craft in the Lowcountry. Native Americans traveled on canoes throughout the region, as had many enslaved Africans on the coast and rivers of West Africa. Both groups had canoe-building traditions. Canoes allowed enslaved people access to the waterways and swamps for fishing and hunting, necessary activities for their subsistence. Canoes, along with flats, were essential craft on rice plantations in moving through the canals of the rice fields.[26]

John Lawson made a memorable canoe passage through the Santee Delta in 1701, and chronicled the trip in *A New Voyage to Carolina*. The canoe utilized was "large," and was big enough to carry a crew of ten "six English-men in Company, with three Indian-men, and one Woman, Wife to our Indian–Guide." They departed Charleston traveling through the creeks and bays along the mainland, and at the end of the first week, entered the mouth of the Santee River. Lawson noted the "fresh water, occasion'd by the extraordinary Current that comes down continually. With hard Rowing, we got two Leagues up the River." In his description of the following day, Lawson again noted the strong current "caus'd us to make small Way with our Oars. With hard Rowing, we got that Night to Mons. Eugee's House, which stands about fifteen Miles up the River, being the first Christian dwelling we met withal in that Settlement, and were very courteously receiv'd by him and his Wife." "Eugee" was Daniel Huger, whose plantation, Watahan, was at the mouth of Wambaw Creek on the South Santee River.[27]

The dugout canoe could be built on-site efficiently and cheaply. The slave narrative of Charles Ball illustrates the relative ease and speed of the construction. Because of Ball's prior experience fishing in Maryland, his owner took him from fieldwork on a South Carolina plantation along with several other enslaved men. They relocated to the plantation's property along the Congaree River in order to start a fishery as a moneymaking venture for the plantation owner. When the master's son set them up with a couple of skiffs for that work, Ball rejected the craft outright due to their decrepit condition. Along with his five peers, Ball completed the construction of two suitable dugouts for this fishery in less than a week, utilizing the large pine trees on site.[28]

Lawson described an improved canoe-like craft. Observing the vast "Ciprus-Trees" (cypress), he described how the French would make vessels out of these huge trees that could "carry fifty or sixty barrels. After the tree is moulded and dug, they saw them in two Pieces, and so put a Plank between, and a small Keel, to preserve them from the Oyster-Banks, which are innumerable in the Creeks and Bays betwixt the French Settlement and Charles-Town. They carry two Masts, and Bermuda sails, which makes them very handy and fit for their Purpose." Lawson was writing of the periagua, a hybrid craft constructed in colonial times containing elements of both the simple Native American craft and European influences including form, propulsion, and rig. Considering the number of crew on Lawson's historic journey, that craft perhaps was a periagua. Periaguas had different capabilities than dugout canoes and rice flats. They could carry larger cargoes than dugouts, had a greater range, and could move swiftly whether under sail or when rowed.[29]

Another type of watercraft in the rice planter's fleet was the schooner. These larger vessels demanded a higher level of building expertise as compared to other plantation craft. A number of the Santee Delta planters owned schooners including Isaac Mazyck (his schooner was captured by a Spanish privateer in 1747); *Charlotte,* William Lucas; *Wambaw*, Henry Laurens (jointly owned with John Coming Ball); *Active*, Daniel Horry and Paul Trapier; *Elizabeth*, Noah Serré (minor) and widow Catherine Serré; *Huzza*, Daniel McGregor; and *Necessity*, John Woodberry and Jonah Collins. These vessels plied the Inland Passage, connecting the Santee with Charleston and farther south by creeks and bays, but also went offshore to make coastal passages. The schooner rig allowed a small crew to handle the vessel. These schooners provided the transport of rice and other plantation products to town, the supply of plantation necessities, and the movement of people including enslaved laborers to and from the plantation.[30]

As the rice plantations became more productive, particularly due to tidal irrigation, planters sought new methods to increase efficiency preparing the raw rice. Market preparation of rice required several processes including threshing, removing the rice from the plant; and milling, removing the hull, bran, and germ from the inner rice. Prior to the development of new technologies, the work was slow and labor intensive; the flail was used in threshing, and the mortar and pestle for milling. The use of mortar and pestle was an ancient and ubiquitous milling process employed in West Africa, as Judith Carney noted, "With the dawn of each day women's pounding of rice awakens millions of African villagers, the rhythmic striking of rice grains by the pestle providing the steady heartbeat of community life."[31]

Water-powered mills had processed grains for thousands of years in the Old World. Jonathan Lucas, an English immigrant millwright, built a number of mills in the Santee Delta, and his sons William and Jonathan Jr. continued in this business. Two main sources of "the command of water" used by water-powered mills were rain-fed reservoirs and tidal freshwater rice fields; Lucas employed both. He built his first mill on the Santee at Peachtree Plantation for John Bowman in 1787, and continued construction in the Delta with the following mills: Millbrook Plantation for Andrew Johnston in 1791, Rice Hope for Edward Crook in 1791, Blake's Plantation (Washo) for Frances Middleton in 1792, Hopsewee for John Hume in 1792, Wambaw Plantation for the estate of Daniel Horry in 1792, and Fairfield Plantation for Thomas Pinckney in 1795. Planters lauded Lucas for his skill and impressive results and sought his enterprise throughout the Lowcountry for mill building. He was a mechanical genius, and earlier efforts by others to improve his rice mill were unsuccessful. In the 1830s, steam power became a more reliable power source for rice milling.[32]

The flourishing of rice culture in the Lowcountry and notably in the Santee Delta produced for the propertied elite a level of wealth not matched in the Southeast. The disparate endeavors of rice planting and gold mining both produced riches. In the 1760s Dr. George Milligen described the inland and tidal properties as the "Golden Mines of Carolina"; "cypress, river, and cane swamps [were the] source of infinite Wealth, and will always reward the industrious and persevering planter." The architect Robert Mills, during a visit to Fairfield Plantation in 1821, described the view of the rice fields as "those gold mines of the state." This analogy may be extended to the fatalities of both rice fields and gold mines. The most successful men in the Rice Kingdom were known as grandees, and the Delta planter Elias Horry IV (1773–1834) could easily claim that status. He accumulated his wealth with large amounts of property, measured in both rice field acreage and numbers of slaves (775). The emergence of rice as a valuable export crop was a function of the planters' command of water. This water management only occurred with planters' orchestration of large populations of enslaved laborers commanded by overseers and slave drivers. The Golden Age of Rice between 1800 and 1860 saw the making of fortunes for the rice elite, elevating Charleston and the South Carolina Lowcountry to the wealthiest area of British North America. This ascendance came to an abrupt end as the nation entered the Civil War.[33]

• CHAPTER •

WAMBAW

The creek cuts a channel through the cypress-gum forest draining the swamp into the waters of the South Santee River. This waterway is one of the many tributaries of the Santee, including a number in the Santee Delta: Echaw, Wahaw, Washaw. All have the "aw" suffix, names given by indigenous peoples without written language. This Santee tributary, Wambaw Creek, and its adjacent lands are distinctive for several reasons. It drains a locally large watershed, the Wambaw swamp. The ecosystem attracted many settlers due to its agricultural potential, and those people and associated events have left a vibrant history. The present Wambaw swamp gives us a glimpse into the primeval Santee Swamp in the Delta.

One historic group of indigenous people, the Sewees, had a settlement along the South Santee somewhere to the east of the Wambaw Creek mouth, and the place became known to colonists as "ye Plantation of King Jeremy." "King Jeremy" was the leader of the Sewees. King Jeremy's Plantation is a European description of a leader "King" and the lands and village "Plantation" where he resided. The exact location of this Native American village remains a mystery. Its site was most likely the reason that the Huguenot settlements along the Santee were dispersed west of the mouth of Wambaw starting with the property of

Daniel Huger, a plantation known by the Native American place name Watahan. Since Huger located his plantation a distance from any of the early Huguenot settlers, it is possible that he was trading with the Sewees just to the east. And this was the "Mons. Eugee's house" where the Englishman John Lawson and his party spent the night as they paddled up the Santee.[1]

Though Huguenots had found their way to the colony beginning in 1680, the revocation of the Edict of Nantes in 1685 led to an increased Huguenot emigration to Carolina seeking religious freedom. Eventually, the colony had the highest percentage of the French population of the thirteen colonies. The Lords Proprietors, who the Crown had granted the charter, did extensive marketing for the new colony, and pamphlets found their way into Huguenot enclaves in France. Many Huguenots obtained grants to vacant lands along the Santee River, at that time the northern boundary of the colony. Settlement of French Santee began in earnest in 1687 with a group of fifty French men leaving Charleston to clear forest for their new town, Jamestown. In the following year, they acquired sites along the Santee east to Wambaw Creek. The settlers noted that their early interactions with Sewee Indians were positive, "all kindness and timidity and, far from having to fear them, they serve us extremely well."[2]

People sought property along Wambaw Creek deep into the swamp due to the land's agricultural fecundity. In the early eighteenth century, inland-swamp culture or reservoir culture was the standard irrigation method for rice cultivation. Huguenots were in a position to recognize and acquire these lands for rice production along with harvesting the forest resources. Besides Daniel Huger, other Huguenot families with early acquisition of land on Wambaw Creek were Horry, Perdriau, St. Julien, Gendron, Peyre, Chastaigner, and Mazyck.

Following Daniel Huger, the immigrant Elie Horry developed another early Wambaw plantation after purchasing a grant to five hundred acres on the east side of Wambaw Creek in 1709. In 1704, Horry married Huger's eldest child, Margueritte Huger. The union was just one example of the intertwining of families by marriage and land both in and out of the Huguenot community. Horry's property became known as Wambaw Plantation, the first of several sites given this name on the creek. The Horrys added other lands on the east side of Wambaw Creek and to the east on the South Santee. One of these properties on the Santee River became Hampton Plantation, the home of Daniel Huger Horry, Elie's grandson.[3]

Wambaw Plantation was the location of one of Jonathan Lucas's rice mills. This plantation included the island formed by the Santee River, Wambaw, and Wahaw Creeks (Wahaw is now known as Hampton Creek). The damming of another creek running through the property created the reserve for running the mill.

Lucas's son William purchased Wambaw Plantation in 1832 to add to a number of his properties in the Santee Delta including Murphy Island (formerly known as Horry Island). William was a mill builder like his father, and he expanded his enterprise to include rice cultivation. Wambaw had extensive pinelands, and Lucas utilized the excellent timber to build the house at his South Santee River home plantation, which became known as the Wedge.[4]

We effortlessly cruised on our watery path through the swamp forest flanking the Santee Delta. Newly emerging spring foliage dappled the forested sides of the waterway and reflected on the creek's surface: cypresses, maples, oaks. A destination awaited us in the Delta: Wambaw Plantation, one of the many historic plantations in the Rice Kingdom. As twenty-first century explorers, armed with an early nineteenth century plat and permission from the owner to visit, Ian Sanchez and I paddled in both familiar waters and toward unknown lands on our quest.

We reached our destination, Wambaw Plantation, which was originally owned by the Horrys. The land has a prominent high bluff on Wambaw Creek, and we scrambled up the bank to begin our exploration. The plat illustrated various structures: a main house and outbuildings, rice mill, and two slave streets with numerous slave dwellings. We did not know what to expect, and our search revealed only traces of the past structures, including a prominence for the main house site, a live oak-lined "street," and scattered brick rubble. Water features included an outlet to the Santee and a "Reserve" listed on the plat. The outlet bisected the dike, so we re-embarked in the canoe and paddled around to access the eastern side of the property. The manmade dike extended some distance to the east and had a natural path on its ridge, kept open it seemed by wildlife. This bank separated the tidal from the reserve waters. No sign remained of the water-run rice mill built by Jonathan Lucas, but the elements for the power were all there. A wheel hub, a metal artifact of the mill, is on display at the Village Museum in McClellanville.

The Delta contains its own archipelago of islands bounded by numerous waterways. The islands and creeks have changed names through history—Watahan to Manigault to Chicken Creek. We touched on one of these Delta islands, now known as Hampton Island, and once part of Wambaw Plantation. Half of this island is the property of the Francis Marion National Forest. These lands, deforested for the creation of rice fields, are now reverting to swamp forest. Signs of recent "plowing" from feral hogs disturbed the ground. We paddled back into Wambaw and through the swamp with the last of the incoming flow, following centuries of paddlers passing through on multiple missions: camping, hunting, exploring, settling, fleeing. These waters and lands hold innumerable mysteries. Many questions remained, and the swamp held on to its secrets; our business was unfinished.

The canoe trip to Wambaw Plantation was one of a number I have made on Wambaw Creek. Wambaw Creek Wilderness in Francis Marion National Forest is a popular venue for paddlers to access the Wambaw swamp. Two local outfitters provide guided kayaking trips in Wambaw Creek, and several landings allow access.

My first experience on Wambaw dates back to a 1980s excursion. With a fellow canoe voyager, Rand Schenck, we put in at the Highway 45 Bridge, and paddled downstream in the upper Wambaw. Our two-day trip ended on the South Santee River near Highway 17. We were fortunate to find accessible high ground for our one-night camping along the creek. My canoe partner was unimpressed with the physical size of the Wambaw Creek Wilderness as set out on our map. His West Coast residence had allowed him to experience extensive wilderness areas. My view of Wambaw was as a wilderness corridor, surrounding the paddler in the swamp environment with little intrusion from the outside world. I experienced this first trip in a blackwater swamp as magnificent and serene.

Spring comes early to the swamp. The microclimate contributes to a number of trees leafing out earlier than upland areas. Wambaw Creek is a powerful draw for people to witness that early spring foliage. The best way to take in the display is on a paddling craft, quietly moving over the tannin-stained waters to view what seems an infinite variety of green hues. In early morning, those same dark waters present a mirror surface reflecting the verdant leaves and sky in a sublime exhibition. Other colors complement the greens, as in the crimsons of red maples. Birds extend the color palette. Wood ducks often play "chase" with paddlers, keeping a steady margin ahead but still allowing a view of their brilliant multicolored plumage. One of the warblers, the prothonotary, flies low through the swamp forest, a dazzling splash of sunlight. Yet to my eye, the emeralds of new cypress needles reign supreme in colorful beauty.

Wambaw Creek, one of the many tributaries of the Santee River. It flows into the South Santee River in the Santee Delta.

The first French Huguenot settlers lived an extremely hard life in the Santee wilderness. One young woman, Judith Giton, described the difficulties of clearing and grubbing out land: "I have been laboring for six months at a time in this country without tasting bread, laboring meanwhile like a slave in tilling the ground." Despite all the pressing needs for these families, they also sought the means to practice their Protestant faith. To receive governmental support to provide funds for ministers and buildings, the Huguenots joined the Church of England. These French Santee Huguenots petitioned the South Carolina Commons House of Assembly to become a parish, and in 1706 the parish of St. James on Santee River was established. The original place of worship was near the site of present-day Jamestown up the Santee River west of the Santee Delta. As Huguenots settled more land to the east on the Santee and up Echaw and Wambaw Creeks, they searched for a more convenient location, and in 1710 built a church at Echaw. In those early days, a bilingual pastor often conducted services in French and English. On lands originally granted to Daniel Horry as part of his Wambaw Plantation, builders completed a more substantial building to the east of Wambaw Creek in 1768. This fourth building of the parish's churches, St. James Santee, became known as the Wambaw Church to distinguish it from the Echaw church, which continued to serve the local community as a chapel of ease.[5]

Driving to the church in 2020 transported me back to an earlier time of travel. The old Georgetown Highway is a narrow two-lane dirt, sand, and mud track through miles of pinelands. On a mid-March day, the recent deluge of rain had resulted in a roadway torn apart by traffic and pockmarked intermittently with holes, ruts, and soggy patches. The old Georgetown Highway was part of the colonial period King's Highway, historically used as a path by those on foot, on horseback, and on carts. As I approached the church site, the pinelands opened up to a human oasis in a woodland wilderness. The church predates the birth of the United States, and maintains the beauty of the Georgian design and artisan craftsmanship. Local longleaf pine and cypress provided framing, finish trim, and pews. Builders used brick as the predominant construction material, and fashioned round brick columns supporting the portico on the southeast and northwest sides.

A closer look at the column brickwork reveals master craftsmanship. Builders imported English bricks for the building's walls and brick pavers for the flooring, but site-made, wedge-shaped bricks compose the columns. About five feet above the ground, the columns taper to their apex requiring the wedge-shaped bricks to change in size in their ascent. The molds for making the brick would therefore have changed, requiring a difficult process to manufacture this tapering detail. While the brickwork stands out, the cornice-work creates the transition between the brick walls and the metal roof, also making an impression on this observer, who in the past helped build a cornice around the top of a four-story university building in Wilmington, North Carolina. While this edifice stands only one story, the challenges of acquiring the local materials, milling the various moldings without power tools, and rising to the cornice height to fashion the architectural detail provoked some questions. Who designed this structure? Who were the artisans, and how did they learn their trades? Did they reside at the site during construction? What were some of the challenges of the construction process in this isolated location?

The building has come to be known as "Brick Church." A recently constructed brick wall surrounding the church and graveyard complements the one-story brick building. A number of notable persons are interred in the graveyard, including Jonah Collins, Reverend Samuel Fenner Warren, Jack Leland, and Peter Manigault. One grave marker, a sandstone obelisk relocated from his Santee Delta plantation, memorializes a prominent Huguenot immigrant, Daniel Huger. Born in 1651 in France, he emigrated to South Carolina in 1685, and died in 1715 at Wambaw. He was the same "Mr. Eugee" with whom John Lawson spent a night at Watahan in 1701.[6]

Brick Church lies off the beaten path. The structure is hidden to the typical traveler but invites a visit. The once vibrant rural community of Wambaw in 1768 is gone; it is now a church in the wilderness.

Theodore Gaillard (1714–1781) was one of the sons of Barthélémy Gaillard, the Huguenot immigrant. Theodore arrived in 1687 with his parents and settled with them and his two brothers at French Santee. Gaillard went on to serve in the Commons House of Assembly. He married other Huguenots; his first marriage was to Elizabeth Serré, and his second to Lydia Peyre. Two of the properties listed in his will were in Wambaw. The first was on the west side of Wambaw Creek upstream from the the South Santee, and known as "Bruneau Old Field." "Old field" was a description often listed on plats as open areas formerly cultivated by Indians. The second property described by Gaillard on the will was the "plantation where I now live."[7]

Two weddings in the 1760s took place in Gaillard's "dwelling-house" at this Wambaw plantation. In 1762 his eldest daughter Elizabeth married the widower Job Marion, the brother of Francis Marion. Francis Marion and Elizabeth's younger sister Catherine were witnesses for the ceremony. Three years later in the same house, Catherine would marry Elias Ball, who had inherited a share of his father's (John Coming Ball) Wambaw Plantation in 1764 upon his death. Two of Theodore's brothers, Tacitus and Alcimus, also had plantations on Wambaw Creek.[8]

John Coming Ball secured the large property to be known as Wambaw Plantation as one of a number of acquisitions. He married Catherine Gendron, whose father (John II) and grandfather (Philippe, a Huguenot immigrant) were large landholders in French Santee. Ball purchased this property from his father-in-law. After the death of Catherine in 1755, he married another Huguenot descendant, Judith Boisseau, and they lived on their Cooper River plantation, Hyde Park. Wambaw Plantation was a business venture, and Ball developed a partnership with his brother-in-law Henry Laurens, who had married Ball's half-sister Eleanor in 1750. Laurens purchased a one-half interest in Ball's Wambaw Plantation in 1756, and this land ownership qualified Laurens to run for election in the South Carolina Commons House of Assembly. He was elected to the Assembly in 1757, an event that began a political career that saw him elected as president of the Continental Congress twenty years later. Laurens would go on to purchase seven other large properties in South Carolina and Georgia.[9]

By the time of the Wambaw purchase, Laurens had already achieved tremendous success and wealth as a merchant. A partner in this business was George Austin, who had also married a sister of John Coming Ball. They imported rum and produce from the West Indies, manufactured goods from England, and enslaved Africans; they exported naval stores, deerskins, rice, indigo, and other products from South Carolina. Laurens's business move to plantation ownership was outside his expertise, and he relied on Ball's experience as a planter. They pooled their resources for this plantation enterprise: management, a contingent of slaves owned by each, and the ownership of a vessel, the schooner *Wambaw*. Neither Ball nor Laurens lived at Wambaw, and they employed a resident overseer managing the day-to-day activities of the plantation. Their Wambaw Plantation would not fit the mythic mold of the southern plantation with big house and resident owners; it was more in line with what historian Peter Wood described as a "slave labor camp." We can attribute much of what we know of this Wambaw Plantation from the voluminous correspondence and bookkeeping of Laurens and the preservation of those papers.[10]

The most lucrative product at Wambaw was rice, which averaged over 90 percent of the sales. There were smaller productions of shingles and corn. During Laurens's ownership, almost eighty of his slaves resided at Wambaw; Ball probably had the same number. Laurens's correspondence often included complaints about his employees and slaves, and their impact on the bottom line. He noted in a letter to Ball how their schooner *Wambaw* was not ready to pick up rice for transport due to "the Patroon might if he pleased have Sailed 2 or 3 days before Christmas, but he had chalked out to keep his Holydays in Charles Town at a very great expence to you & me." The letters to his overseers at Wambaw gave evidence of Laurens's micromanagement of the plantation's affairs. In one letter to his Wambaw overseer Abraham Schad, Laurens made various complaints and directions. "Why did you not ask this when I was with you? ...You are very forgetful in omitting to mention the Article of Beef when I was at Wambaw & now you ask what you must do. ...Let me know this & then I shall answer you, which might have been done better by voice, for you hate writing & will never write enough. . . . The Taylor now goes to finish cutting the Negro Cloths in which be very frugal . . . pray let no waste be committed. . .The Taylor will probably be able to come away on Friday. Don't detain him an hour. He is too expensive a guest."[11]

In the same years, Laurens continued to be involved in transatlantic trade and documented transactions such as selling slaves transported on the ship *Queen of Bara* from Bance (now Bunce) Island in Sierra Leone, and sending mahogany on a return voyage to London on board the same vessel. Ball was the primary manager of Wambaw Plantation until his death in 1764, when his son Elias inherited a portion of this plantation. Laurens unhappily took over the ongoing management for a period of time. As plantation owner, Laurens was responsible for his slaves' food, clothing, health, and shelter. In 1766 Laurens sent the carpenter William Yates to Wambaw, and from a letter to his overseer Abraham Schad it seemed that Yates would be working on slave housing. Laurens instructed Schad, "I do not think it practicable to send up Bricks for the Negro Chimneys. Therefore Wooden ones as usual must serve and & Sam will be with you very soon & assist about the management of Clay to serve instead of Bricks." This directive was certainly a financial decision. Laurens's meticulous bookkeeping allowed him to calculate rates of return on all his plantations. Laurens considered 8 percent rate of return a minimum for profitability. In the three years documented in Laurens's master account book, Wambaw Plantation's rate of return never rose above 9 percent. With limited returns and financial potential for Wambaw, Laurens sold his one-half share in 1769.[12]

In a letter, Laurens responded to an inquiry from another Wambaw neighbor and planter, Paul Douxsaint, who requested water to be released from the "Wambaw Dam." Douxsaint was obviously downstream of Laurens and made this request for irrigation purposes. Laurens was receptive, but with one caveat: "You will be so good as to think not only of the present hour, but also save provision in our Reserve against a dry spell, which may still happen, in this I am persuaded that you will do What is right & therefore shall lay you under no restraint."[13] An advertisement in the *City Gazette* for the sale of "Two Very Valuable Rice Plantations," on November 26, 1787, described "that well known inland rice plantation, on Wambaw, formerly belonging to Elias Ball" (and previously by John Coming Ball and Henry Laurens.) The notice went on to market this plantation as "always esteemed the first inland swamp in the state: It is lately resurveyed and divided into two tracts, reserving to each a compleat command of the water, so that the crops are certain there."[14]

Wambaw was also the name of the schooner co-owned by Henry Laurens and John Coming Ball. *Wambaw* made numerous voyages from Laurens's home base in Charleston, Rattray Green in Ansonborough. *Wambaw* could not navigate Wambaw Creek; one letter of Laurens noted the vessel docking at "the Wambaw Landing," located somewhere along the entrance to Wambaw Creek off the South Santee River, perhaps at the Horry Wambaw Plantation. *Wambaw* carried to Wambaw Plantation and other plantations in his growing empire wide-ranging cargoes, from materials to people.[15]

As Laurens related in his letter to Joseph Brown, a Georgetown merchant, he was sending two runaways, Aaron and James, part of a recently purchased group.

Wambaw with John Gray as master was heading to Winyaw "in hopes of getting some Freight." Laurens sent the two runaways for sale, though Gray was given the option of keeping James for "a Boat Negro for which he was recommended by the Master of Mr. Philp's Boat [Phillips being the captain of the schooner *Thomas*] who brought them to Town." We may infer that Phillips made this recommendation after James had demonstrated boat skills on that earlier trip.[16]

Laurens recorded the value of the *Wambaw* and the plantation in his account book in 1766. He listed the *Wambaw* schooner as worth £1,200, and the crew of five enslaved men on board as £2,000, a total of £3,200. Wambaw Plantation at the same time was valued at £10,000 including "Land. 1,500 acres improv'd with Dam's, Buildings, Cattle, Horses, Hogs, Tools, &Ca." He included "for 79 Negroes as per List at £300 per head," a subtotal of £23,700.[17]

The *Wambaw* would play an outsized role in Laurens's future. Upon its return to Charleston from Laurens's new Georgia plantation, British officials seized the schooner. Laurens took legal action, writing a series of pamphlets attacking this imperial oppression. These writings were widely disseminated throughout the colonies, and exhibited a political shift of the conservative Laurens toward advocating for American independence.

Owned at the time of the Revolutionary War by "Wambaw Elias" Ball, Wambaw Plantation is among the hidden features of the Santee Delta region. Elias Ball (1744–1822) had a number of family members with the same name, and he acquired the moniker "Wambaw Elias" in reference to the plantation where he lived. Although documents recording the plantation's history exist, the plantation's remains had been concealed in the Francis Marion National Forest. Henry Mouzon's *An Accurate Map of North and South Carolina with Their Indian Frontiers* from 1775 showed a Ball plantation in the general area of the Wambaw Swamp at the head of Wambaw Creek, but this small-scale map does not allow a definitive placement. The correspondence of Henry Laurens provided tantalizing clues. An early hunt for maps and plats led to some disappointment when a lack of necessary details thwarted a pinpointing of the Ball Wambaw Plantation.

Working with Robert Morgan, archaeologist and heritage program manager for the Francis Marion and Sumter National Forests, he and I became optimistic about "rediscovering" this site. Morgan accessed from his archives two valuable items: a plat containing details of Wambaw Plantation, and a lidar-generated map of the area. Concurrently I located another detailed plat of Wambaw Plantation at the South Carolina Historical Society. With a strong correlation between these two plats and the features displayed on the lidar map, Morgan was increasingly confident about the plantation's location.

And then there was a surprise find. In 1989 Francis Marion National Forest staff identified a number of potential historic sites after Hurricane Hugo, and contracted the firm Brockington and Associates to investigate the sites. Morgan found their report from 1992, by Jeffery Gardner and Eric Poplin, "Historic Adaptations Through Time: Archaeological Testing of Five Sites, Francis Marion National Forest," pertinent to our search. One of those sites, 38CH1098, proved most promising, and after shovel testing, the Brockington group expanded the study to include more intensive archaeology and archival research. Francis Marion National Forest had originally identified and recorded the site in November 1989 when three brick piles, a possible old roadbed, and a group of large live oak trees stood out. Initial testing unearthed a number of eighteenth-century artifacts, and the search expanded to an area 150 by 130 meters.[18]

The archaeological work at 38CH1098 resulted in the collection of 7,300 artifacts. Of the artifact assemblage 64 percent were colonoware, and their presence strongly suggested the site was a slave settlement. Colonoware is a broad class of pottery associated with historic-period sites. This form of pottery was not made in kilns but rather on open hearths. While Native Americans made some colonoware, enslaved Africans made the majority on plantations, and most likely the Wambaw Plantation colonoware. The mean date for all ceramics was 1752, and the low numbers of whiteware, a nineteenth century ceramic, suggested the abandonment of the site by the early nineteenth century. The archival research confirmed the site as part of the Ball plantation. The United States government purchased the property in 1935 and included it in the Francis Marion National Forest.[19]

The Brockington report recommended 38CH1098 as eligible for listing on the National Register of Historic Places due to both the archaeological and documentary evidence. Interestingly, the three-thousand-acre tract of land covering the entire Ball plantation and divided by the Charleston County/Berkeley County boundary also contained another promising archaeological site, 38BK920. The report speculated these two settlement sites might have been the locations of the John Coming Ball and Henry Laurens properties. Neither of these two owners resided there, but "Wambaw Elias" Ball did, and the report proposed his residence was most likely at 38BK920. The final assessment for 38CH1098 was that it possessed "significant archaeological deposits" and research potential.[20]

In 2020, there were still features from the Brockington report extant: the humus-covered brick piles, a pond (perhaps a borrow pit), and the live oak trees.

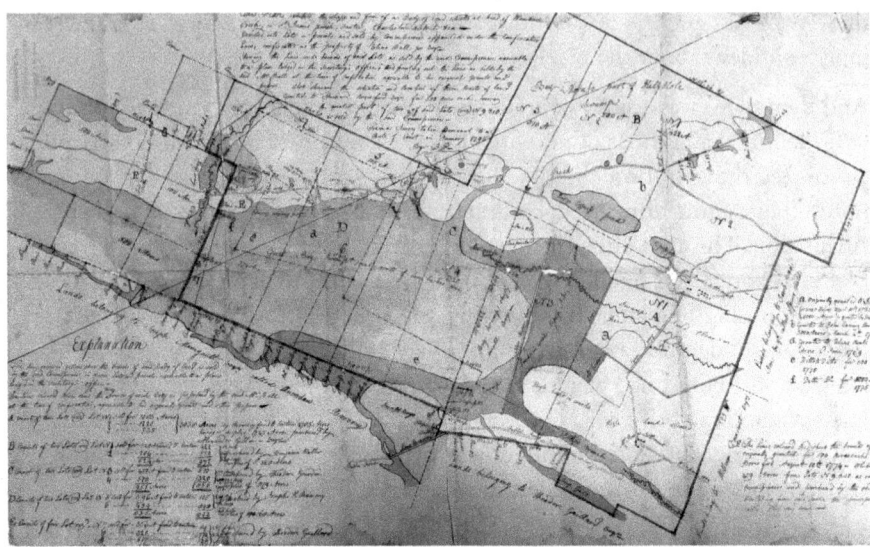

Plat of Wambaw Creek land, Joseph Purcell, 1795.

The site exists next to an unpaved road running through Francis Marion National Forest, and the adjacent uplands are fire-maintained pinelands. To the west lies the Wambaw Swamp Wilderness Area, the wetlands originally transformed to become reservoir irrigated rice fields that have now reverted to cypress-gum forest. The road along the swamp crosses two small bridges over the upper parts of Wambaw Creek, and then past the boundary between Charleston and Berkeley Counties. There is little sign of the enterprise and dramas that took place here in the late eighteenth century.

It would be a stretch to say that this Wambaw Plantation is in the Santee Delta, even within the loose geographic construct of the Delta's extent. The search for its location inevitably moved farther up Wambaw Creek into the upper portions of this watershed. This Wambaw Plantation has a tangible geographic connection to the Delta with the other Wambaw plantations arrayed along the creek banks all the way to the South Santee River. The plantation's watercraft transported needed goods, supplies, and people, and plied the Delta's waters. The owners and residents formed social and marital bonds with other people of the Delta.

Wambaw and its inhabitants would directly experience the Revolutionary War. The fractured families and conflicts created by shifting loyalties of the Wambaw elite support the interpretation of these hostilities as the first Civil War in South Carolina. Elias Ball (1744–1822), "Wambaw Elias", was the firstborn of his father's children and followed his father in marrying into an elite Huguenot family, the Gaillards. The Ball family, like others in the Lowcountry, had conflicting allegiances in the Revolutionary War, and some of those allegiances switched as the war's tide changed. At the fall of Charleston and British occupation of the city, a number of Lowcountry residents made critical decisions. In the Ball family both Wambaw Elias's half-brother John Coming Ball (1758–1792) and his cousin "Third Elias" Ball (1752–1810) switched sides to join the occupation force. Previously in 1775, Third Elias had signed up for a militia led by Job Marion and was elected to a seat in the Provincial Congress in Charleston.[21]

Another member of the family, John Ball (1760–1817), cousin of Wambaw Elias, joined the patriot cause when he signed up for the militia of Daniel Horry's Light Dragoons. This militia leader was Daniel Huger Horry Jr. of Wambaw and Hampton Plantations. The unit was part of the Second Regiment of Provincials under the command of General William Moultrie. Horry changed his allegiance after the fall of Charleston and took his young son Daniel Huger Horry II with him to England for his education. Horry's wife Harriott Pinckney Horry stayed at Hampton managing the plantation's affairs and supporting the rebel cause. Two of Daniel Horry's cousins, Peter and Hugh, served under Francis Marion. John Ball remained a patriot throughout the war and found time during his service to marry his first cousin Jane Ball (1761–1804), the half-sister of Wambaw Elias.[22]

Theodore Gaillard Sr. was a staunch loyalist, and his sons followed his allegiance to the Crown. Lord Charles Cornwallis, the British leader in charge of the southern campaign, noted in a letter to General Henry Clinton that both Theodore Gaillard Jr. (1737–1805) and Wambaw Elias Ball had shown "ardent proofs of their loyalty." Gaillard had helped the movement of supplies from Murray's Ferry on the Santee River to Cornwallis's army at Camden. Ball had survived a patriot attack on his small force at his Wambaw Plantation. Ball fled into the Wambaw Swamp, managed to mount a fast horse, and made the ride to Strawberry Ferry. Meeting up with the British forces there, Ball provided the information necessary for Lieutenant Colonel Banastre Tarleton to intercept and crush a patriot force at Lenud's Ferry on the Santee. Cornwallis was banking on substantial assistance from South Carolina loyalists in England's southern campaign, and he rewarded Gaillard and Ball with commissions as lieutenant colonels in the militia. Cornwallis further charged Ball with leading the raising of the militia in Craven and Berkeley Counties. Wambaw Elias appeared to have inherited the ruthlessness of his grandfather Elias "Red Cap" Ball, the immigrant and patriarch of the Ball family. Another Elias Ball (Third Elias) and Theodore Jr.'s brother John Gaillard (1735–1800) also received British commissions.[23]

Allegiance in the Revolutionary War for Lowcountry residents was not simply rebel or loyalist, particularly after the surrender of Charleston by General Benjamin Lincoln on May 12, 1780. Citizens in town and country were required to sign allegiance to the Crown to receive "protection." Refusal meant imprisonment and property seizure, and over one hundred properties of patriots were seized in September 1780, including those of Henry Laurens, Francis Marion, Peter Horry, and Charles Cotesworth Pinckney.[24]

Loyalties continued to change during the conflict. Theodore Gaillard Sr.'s youngest son, Peter (1757–1833), had his best friend Samuel Dubose choose the patriot side. Most likely due to the influence of his father and his older brothers, Peter joined the Tory militia and served under Wambaw Elias's cousin John Coming Ball (1758–1792) as his second-in-command. Their group of around fifty men was camped at Patrick Dollard's Red Tavern on Black Mingo Creek when a force led by Francis Marion attacked at midnight. Marion's men knew intimately many of the loyalist militia as neighbors, former friends, and family relations. The fight was over quickly; the patriot force routed the loyalist militia who escaped into the nearby swamp. Though John Coming Ball was not captured, his Tory military career was all but over. The rebels took his horse, and it became Marion's mount for the rest of the campaign, humorously named "Ball." The defeat led to soul-searching by Peter Gaillard, and soon after his father's death in 1781 he wrote a letter expressing his desire to join the patriot side in Marion's militia. Marion was receptive, met with Gaillard, and incorporated him into his brigade. Besides his service with Marion, Gaillard went on to serve under General William Moultrie and Colonel John Laurens, witnessing the death of this oldest son of Henry Laurens in the last throes of South Carolina bloodshed.[25]

Both sides in the war utilized enslaved people in the conflict. The British sent Harry, a slave owned by the loyalist Gaillard family, to spy on rebels in the Lowcountry. Governor John Rutledge had directed Francis Marion to execute any slaves spying for the British, and Marion's men caught Harry spying on them near Monck's Corner. The rebels killed Harry, beheaded him, and placed his head on a stake as a warning to other slaves.[26]

Although many of Francis Marion's military campaigns occurred in the lands and swamps between the Santee and Great Pee Dee Rivers, he and his men at times ventured into the Santee Delta. Marion had located one of his swamp camps at the confluence of the South Santee River and Wambaw Creek. In January 1782, the Fourth General Assembly convened in Jacksonboro, and Marion attended. He had traveled from his Wambaw camp and left two of his captains, Peter Horry and Hezekiah Maham, in charge of his militia. An ongoing conflict between the two contributed to a defeat at Wambaw Bridge, a wooden structure crossing Wambaw Creek on the road paralleling the South Santee. Both Horry and Maham were absent, and they had delegated subordinates to take charge. A loyalist force led by Lieutenant Colonel Benjamin Thompson attacked and routed this disorganized segment of Marion's forces. The patriot losses numbered around forty, and the survivors escaped into the Wambaw swamp.[27]

One of the pieces of legislation that the Assembly debated and passed in Jacksonboro was the Confiscation Act of 1782, which specified punishment of a range of citizens who supported the British cause. The debates lasted weeks on this issue of accountability, and Marion sided with the more conciliatory wing. Besides revenge, the Assembly sought to raise revenue for the state through confiscation and auctioning of loyalist estates. The range of penalties included confiscation of property and banishment for the worst offenders, and amercement (12 percent fine) for others. Subsequent pieces of legislation in coming years reduced the number of families penalized and allowed for appeals of the earlier judgments. An accounting was in store for some of the Wambaw loyalist elite.[28]

After the defeat of the British at Yorktown, and prior to the evacuation of the British and abandonment of Charleston, Wambaw Elias and his family resided in Charleston as the British prepared to leave South Carolina. Rumors were afoot that patriots were going to seize slaves at his plantation as property for sale. Wambaw Elias would not suffer this loss without a fight, and he led a group of British cavalry on a ride to Wambaw Plantation to capture these slaves. He had minimal success, since most of the slaves escaped into the swamp. After his return to Charleston, his next strategy was to order his plantation overseer to withhold food in a strategy to have the slaves "surrender," but the overseer did not carry out this inhumane act. The rebel insurgents next made their move at Wambaw, capturing fifty-two Wambaw slaves, transporting them to Georgetown, and raising funds with their sale. Not to be denied, Wambaw Elias traveled again to his property with British troops, captured the remaining one hundred slaves, transported them to his cousin Third Elias' plantation, Comingtee, on the Cooper River, and received a promissory note from him for £8,000. Wambaw Elias and his family, joined by John Gaillard, left Charleston with the British fleet and traveled to Florida.[29]

The rest of the Ball loyalists stayed. Elias Ball (Third Elias) of Comingtee Plantation, Wambaw Elias's cousin, who had purchased the slaves with the promissory note, was relieved of any penalty. While in Florida, both Wambaw Elias and John Gaillard appealed the judgment of the Assembly. After the Assembly rejected their pleas, they traveled to England. They sought compensation in London with the Royal Commission for their lost properties. After the passing of a piece of legislation by the Assembly in 1784, John Gaillard and his brother Theodore Jr. appealed before a Conference Committee in Charleston. The Assembly charged John Gaillard with escorting prisoners, who had refused to take protection, to Charleston for shipment to and imprisonment at St. Augustine. Gaillard presented evidence that the order had come from Wambaw Elias. Several days after the appeal hearing, Gaillard and his brother Theodore had their confiscation and banishment revoked for the less serious penalty of amercement. Wambaw Elias received no such relief and stayed in residence in England for the rest of his life. Wambaw Elias remained a resentful and embittered man. He hounded his cousin for payment for his slaves and sought in correspondence with the patriot John Ball, his cousin and the husband of his half-sister Jane, a higher share from his father's will and inheritance. Wambaw Elias finally received £12,700 as compensation from the British Treasury and additionally a lifetime pension.[30]

At the fall of Charleston, Daniel Huger Horry, cousin of patriots Peter and Hugh Horry, fit the category of reluctant Tory, inwardly siding with the patriot cause but concluded the Revolution was over and sought the best position for his family. He accepted the British oath to the dismay of his brothers-in-law, Thomas and Charles Cotesworth Pinckney. Horry traveled to England and took his only son with him for his education. Since he had made no contribution to the British cause, he and his estate were relieved of amercement. Horry finally returned to South Carolina, but died in 1785. Daniel Huger Horry's son did not return from Europe to take over the large estate he had inherited. He chose to live in France, married a woman from Lafayette's extended family, and changed his name from Daniel Huger Horry Jr. to Charles Lucas Pinckney Horry.[31]

· CHAPTER ·

Terror and Death in the Delta

The night of May 27, 1821, was eventful on South Island in the northeastern corner of the Santee Delta. Several runaway slaves were stealing livestock from the plantation of George Ford. They had been in the neighborhood for some time, perhaps months, living in a secluded camp. Though they had local allies, on this night other slaves alerted Ford to the robbery. With the support of others, Ford set out to intervene, but in the confrontation, he was shot and killed. His death initiated a period of terror and revenge in the Delta and beyond. An ongoing hunt for the leader and identified killer, the infamous runaway Joe also known as Forest, would take over two years and cover a hundred miles along the Santee River.

Who were these runaways? Government documents and newspaper reports provide the lens for viewing the evidence covering Ford's murder and the hunt for Joe. At times false reports of his capture circulated. A proclamation issued by Governor Thomas Bennett outlining a reward for the capture of the two leaders provides a detailed description of the two men.

> Jack, a short thick set, athletic man, black, projecting forehead, dark, heavy and lowering eyebrows. A terrible expression of countenance, about 5 feet 7 inches high; is a Virginian by birth, was brought to this State by a Mr. Sibley and is owned by a Mr. Fonberg of Lancaster district, who lives about fifteen miles from the village. Joe, is of an Indian complexion, has a scar on one of his cheeks, (believed to be the right) occasioned by the bite of a negro in a fight; a scar from the cut of a sabre, believed to be on his right arm; has shot marks in both of his legs, is in the prime of life, a very stout and athletic man, at least six feet high.[1]

It is likely that these descriptions were partially obtained from another enslaved man named Jack, who was owned by "Mrs. Horry" and who had been captured that night on South Island. This same Jack described an episode when Joe reportedly shot at "Mr. McClenan of Santee" (probably Archibald McClennan, Jr.). Jack disputed a report that the gun had snapped; instead McClennan's horse had turned and taken off.[2]

At the time of this proclamation's publication, authorities had captured Jack, Joe's cohort, four days after Ford's death on South Island. A militia led by Captain Henry L. Carnes found and confronted Jack, Joe, and a female companion, wounding the woman and capturing Jack, though Joe made his escape. This Jack from the Midlands received a guilty verdict and death sentence at his trial, and died by hanging on June 8. On June 25, the enslaved Jack owned by Mrs. Horry sustained the same verdict and sentence. But Governor Bennett pardoned him on July 11 and banished him from the state. One may infer that the pardon was the result of information he provided to aid the search for Jack and Joe.[3]

The hunt for Joe continued in earnest in the Santee Delta and up the Santee River. Joe had acquired his nickname Forest through his woodcraft skills and ability to disappear into the recesses of the swamp's forests and canebrakes. The militia spotted Joe as he was paddling a dugout canoe upriver and almost captured him. He abandoned his canoe, provisions, and some of his clothing, and vanished again into the swamp on foot. At one point, two detachments of militia searched for Joe on either side of the Delta. On June 6, 1821, a newspaper reported that Joe had entered the house of a "free man," and at gunpoint took from the female occupant bacon, corn, and ammunition before heading back into the swamp. On June 22, another sighting of Joe occurred at the headwaters of the Sampit River by a resident, Captain William S. Harvey. Harvey observed the smoke from a fire back in the swamp of Gravely Gully, and got a look at a person fitting Joe's description. The next day Harvey noticed the tracks of three men and several items missing from his property: lead from a net, a small canoe, and another boat. A newspaper reported that two days later, Joe robbed a house on Turkey Creek. Other reports of Joe's presence late in 1821 proved to be false.

One account in October stated he was seen back up on the Wateree and was "mortally wounded." Another report of his capture near Stateburg also was not true, and his trail as followed in various newspapers seemed to disappear until the following fall.[4]

As noted in Governor Bennett's proclamation, Joe and Jack, along with others, had set up camp for some months in the neighborhood of Ford's plantation on South Island. The document described two other camps, one at the fork of the Congaree and Wateree Rivers, and a second further up the Wateree River. These camps were maroon communities or settlements and populated with runaways. Joe was the head of these settlements, and descriptions of his eventful history often cited his leadership skills. The location of the camps fit a pattern of other maroon settlements in the Southeast. The river systems in the Lowcountry and Piedmont encompassed a great expanse of wetlands, and the transformation of the Lowcountry swamps to tidal rice impoundments occurred along the rivers. These swamps also extended further into a wilderness of swamp and floodplain forest. These "back swamps" became fertile territory for slaves to exploit in subsistence hunting and fishing, and in efforts to "steal themselves" in their flight from slavery. The exploits of Joe revealed an individual familiar with the vast Santee River system and knowledgeable in traveling and surviving in these swamps.[5]

*African American men hiding in a swamp in Louisiana,
a scene similar to antebellum South Carolina maroon camps.*

The killing of George Ford and the continuing presence of Joe and the danger he represented pervaded the Lowcountry and beyond. His defiance and "depredations" kindled fear of a more widespread insurrection modeled on what occurred in Saint-Domingue in the 1791 slave revolt. The excitement of Lowcountry Blacks in response to that Revolution was not lost on Whites, and slave owners made a concerted effort to suppress this news. Such a news blackout was a difficult objective since the fleeing planters from Saint-Domingue brought along their slaves who were already "infected with the disease of liberty." Increasing the level of fear was the fact that the enslaved represented a large majority: within the Georgetown District in 1820, 88 percent of the population was African American. The terror of slave revolts in the Lowcountry had other historical roots. In 1739 whites crushed the Stono Rebellion, a Lowcountry slave insurrection, but the threat was not forgotten. Leading up to the clash for independence with England, rumors about the British inciting a slave rebellion to aid the Crown stoked anxiety. The actions of the Virginia royal governor, Lord Dunmore, in proclaiming that slaves taking up arms against the rebellion would win their freedom, added fuel to the fire. Runaway slaves began fleeing to Sullivan's Island, and a small British fleet nearby raised the hope for freedom. A maroon community developed with thatched huts around the Pest House, where imported slaves were quarantined upon coming into Charleston.[6]

Another major threat to the white minority in the Lowcountry came to light in the summer of 1822. A slave told his owner of an impending slave insurrection, and after further corroboration authorities arrested a number of enslaved men and several free blacks, most notably the alleged leader, Denmark Vesey. The initial date for the planned insurrection was July 14, 1822. It was reported that recruits to the insurrection numbered nine thousand blacks from the Lowcountry, and recruiters had traveled to the Santee on several occasions. Their "trusted" slaves' participation blindsided a number of slave owners, none with more humiliation than Governor Thomas Bennett, author of the 1821 proclamation advertising rewards for Joe and Jack. Authorities arrested and convicted three of Bennett's slaves—Ned, Rolla, and Batteau—who were hung in the first group of six including Vesey on July 2, 1822. One of the Santee planters, Elias Horry IV (1773–1834), owner of over seven hundred slaves, was incredulous at the arrest of his trusted coachman John for participation in the conspiracy. When the arresting officer presented evidence, and Horry asked John to respond, the coachman answered that if the plot had succeeded, he planned "to kill you, to rip open your belly, and throw the guts in your face." Authorities hung John in the second group of convicted on July 12, 1822, along with perhaps Vesey's most important lieutenant, Gullah Jack Pritchard. Pritchard had traveled to the Santee plantations as a recruiter.[7]

Authorities took a number of measures to remove the threat of future insurrections. A debate ensued between the opinion that stricter laws would cause more problems and the opposing view that indulgence of slaves made matters worse. The government strived to enforce an existing ordinance in Charleston prohibiting the teaching of both enslaved and free blacks to read or write. The Assembly passed the Negro Seamen Act on December 22, 1822, which required all vessels entering South Carolina ports with black seamen to send them to jail until the ship's departure, in an effort to restrict communication between those sailors and local blacks. The banishing of the leadership of the African Methodist Episcopal (AME) Church, including Morris Brown from South Carolina, the dissolution of the congregations, and the demolition of the Hampstead AME Church in the fall of 1822, addressed the role of religion in the planned insurrection. In July 1823, a group of Lowcountry planters formed the South Carolina Association, a voluntary organization to enforce the stricter slave codes.[8]

Others placed the blame for the planned revolt on the abolitionist movement in the North. The debate about the admission of Missouri into the Union and the status of slavery in this new state made the existence of slavery a national topic. Whites and blacks in the Lowcountry followed this news, and the states' rights advocate Robert Turnbull asserted that these debates triggered the beginning of slave unrest in the Lowcountry. In one of many pamphlets written in the aftermath of the Vesey conspiracy trial, Thomas Pinckney, diplomat and Santee Delta planter, targeted the reason for the plot as "indiscreet zeal of universal liberty, expressed by many of our fellow-citizens in the States north and east of Maryland." There remained a lingering feeling expressed by Charlestonian Martha Proctor Richardson who "fear[ed another] such an attempt will one day be made." Another woman noted, "I have heard it remarked by several that all confidence in them [domestic servants] is forever at an end."[9]

The whites' anxiety only increased fear in the black community. One concern was the breaking up of enslaved families if sold to different owners, a result that often occurred after the death of an owner and dispersal of the estate. The possibility of sale to a more brutal owner increased the likelihood of harsher discipline. For families split up but living within some proximity, making visits ran the risk of capture by slave patrols and subsequent punishment. Runaways had even stronger deterrents if captured and sent to the Charleston Workhouse, where professionals doled out punishment, including whippings and placement in a human treadmill for grinding grain.[10]

The Revolutionary War had opened up the possibility of freedom for the enslaved, and plantation organization and discipline had degraded. After the war, slave owners made a concerted effort to restore their dominion with the use of overwhelming force. Insubordination and defiance were ongoing problems that masters had to deal with, and to bolster the plantation system they had to demonstrate "a willingness to employ terror." Planters knew that many enslaved individuals were not submissive, and the high numbers of runaways reinforced the idea that some slaves would take extreme risks to remove themselves from their subjugated status.[11]

The schooner *William* out of Boston departed on September 25, 1822, from St. Marys, Georgia, with a load of lumber heading north for Philadelphia. Two days later and twenty miles south of Savannah, a massive storm overtook her with winds that capsized the vessel. After the schooner lay on its side for thirty minutes, the crew cut the weather lanyards to the masts, and the hull righted. Waves washed the entire crew off the deck: Captain Richard Allen, mate James Watson, S. Ames, S. Allen, J. Echleston, J. Parsons, J. N. Jones, and "a black boy." All regained the deck except for Jones, who was drowned. The hull was full of water, and for ten days they survived on the wreck with a small amount of rationed food, a shark they caught, and limited water. During this time, four vessels passed but did not render assistance. On October 7, the schooner *Eliza and Polly* out of Havana took them off the wreck and headed for Charleston. In a Charleston newspaper report, they thanked Captain Forsyth for the rescue "when they had little hopes of escaping a watery grave."[12]

The storm, known as the Great Gale of 1822, surprised other ships along the coast of Georgia and South Carolina. This storm was more than a gale, and modern meteorologists would classify it as a major hurricane. The havoc wreaked on shipping became more intense on its approach to the South Carolina coast. The log of the United States revenue schooner *Gallatin* contained precise observations from their location riding out the storm in the lee of Bull Island on the night of September 27, 1822. Around midnight the winds had increased to a "perfect hurricane," and the vessel dragged despite having three anchors out. At 2:00 a.m. "she struck on an oyster bank, where, after splitting open the head of the rudder, she was aground. Suddenly the wind, which was now at South, died away, and it remained calm for about ten minutes – It then shifted to S.W. and instantly began to roar with full as much, if not more violence than before." These observations charted the storm's path in its crossing over land on the southern end of Bulls Bay, which exposed the Santee Delta to the north to the storm's extreme destructive sector.[13]

The Great Gale's northeast quadrant not only brought the strongest winds of this major hurricane but also the highest storm surge. The islands between the North and South Santee Rivers had a limited elevation relative to the normal high tides. These low islands were the sites of a number of slave settlements adjacent to the rice fields. Besides the barrier islands of South, Murphy, and Cedar Islands and their enslaved populations, other settlements between the rivers included Crow Island, Fannymeade, Blackwood, Wicklow, and Tranquility. In the aftermath of the hurricane, local newspapers revealed the destruction to life and property. The impact on Murphy Island was most deadly; the rice plantation on this barrier island was part of the properties of Mrs. Harriott Pinckney Horry, and almost fifty of her enslaved people were killed. Murphy's white overseer, Mr. Johnson, was the only survivor from his family.[14]

A North Santee letter detailed the larger tragedy in the Delta: "The loss of lives on the river as far as has come within my knowledge is, of the estate of Ford 1, Robert Huggins 12, C Huggins 26, C.C. Pinckney 4, Mr. Hume 23, Mrs. Horry 46, Mr. Henry Deas 3, Mr J. Middleton 3, Mr. Lynch Horry 4, and five whites." The same letter writer had run into "a number of the Hampton negroes returning from Murphy's Island, who told me that they had been down, and buried 46

Impoundment on Murphy Island.

of Mrs. Horry's Negroes." No firsthand accounts from any enslaved individuals survive; one may only imagine the terror that the residents of the low-lying islands experienced as the winds continued to increase, and the deadly storm surge arrived in the middle of the night. The Great Gale of 1822 appeared to match the intensity of Hurricane Hugo in 1989, the latter's storm "ground zero" coming ashore a little south of the Delta.[15]

The Great Gale also devastated buildings and crops in the Santee Delta. Colonel Vanderhost received word that "your plantation here is in a state of ruin from the storm last night – the barn and corn house are blown down – the dwelling house is unroofed and only five negro houses (out of 25) left – fences blown down and the water has covered all the rice in the field, and in the barn yard – the mill partly unshingled." The storm destroyed the mill of another Santee Delta planter, Mr. Shoolbred. Various accounts described the financial losses due to the destruction of the rice crop. Along the shore of Murphy and Cedar Islands, the storm destroyed the houses that served as summer retreats for the planting elite from the deadly diseases of the rice swamps, and this loss led to the eventual development of a new summer resort, the village of McClellanville.[16]

Estimates of the value of enslaved people to a slave owner's total wealth range from 60 to 66 percent. One of the consequences of the storm was the construction of buildings designed to provide protection from storm surges for slaves living in the Delta. Workers built at least five of these structures, known as storm towers, on the islands between the North and South Santee Rivers. These buildings appear to be unique to the Santee Delta. The towers had a circular brick wall ranging from twenty to thirty feet in diameter, stood about twenty feet tall, and had conical roofs. Stairs allowed shelter-seekers to climb to the floor positioned ten feet above ground. Two towers survive to this day. Bill Mace, during his time as manager of the Santee Coastal Reserve, recalled a day when he thwarted attempts by boaters to take bricks from two sites, one a storm tower, and the other a house chimney. Brick thieves in the Santee Delta have operated for many years and destroyed many cultural resources. Phil Wilkinson recalled an entrepreneur paying thieves $1 per brick and then reselling each to tourists for $5.[17]

I accompanied a Huguenot descendant on my first trip to see the Murphy Island storm tower. There was no dock or pier to land in approaching the tower. I was astounded by this remnant from the nineteenth century. Murphy Island is dominated by wetlands, and little high ground exists for building. The growth of shrubs, vines, and trees has swallowed the remains of this round structure, encompassing a diameter of thirty feet. Trees pushing up from the tower's interior have risen above the walls. The lack of conservation of this remarkable structure was stunning and sad. Bricks were missing in places, and these gaps were the signs of the work of brick thieves and the vulnerability of this building. The isolation of the Murphy Island tower is both a blessing and a curse; it is off the beaten path, but the structure is without protection or surveillance most of the time.

This storm tower deserves to be a conserved and protected memorial. Such a designation would memorialize the many lives lost during the Great Gale of 1822, particularly the almost fifty enslaved people residing on this barrier island who most likely are buried somewhere on the high ground of Murphy. Undoubtably, enslaved laborers worked on raising the walls of the tower. This monument would also recall the institution of slavery itself, and the enslaved people on Murphy Island and in the Santee Delta who lived, worked, and died here.

Brick remains of round storm tower on Murphy Island.

Joe's trail had grown cold until a report in November 1822 described how he had returned to Mrs. Horry's plantation. Authorities discovered and chased him all the way to Vance's ferry (now under the waters of Lake Marion). Pursuers captured two of his companions, but once again Joe remained at large. It was not until August 1823 that authorities learned of his whereabouts. He and several companions came onto the plantation of a Colonel Richardson near the fork of the Congaree and Wateree Rivers, and Joe killed the driver, a slave belonging to Richardson. This act was described as a revenge killing relating to a woman.

Not long after this action, the Pineville Police Association formed to take matters into their own hands to find and eliminate Joe and his gang, who had also been operating in their neighborhood. An enslaved man, Royal, was promised his freedom if he assisted the group in finding Joe. With his help, on October 4, 1823, a contingent from this association surprised and killed Joe and three companions near the locks of the Santee Canal connecting with the Santee. As a warning to other slaves, authorities decapitated Joe and placed his head on a pike. In the coming days, the group assaulted the maroon base, wounded one inhabitant, and killed a three-year-old child. The next day, their pursuit tracked down the fleeing runaways from the camp and killed, captured, and wounded several, including Dinah or Diannah, reported to be Joe's wife. The confrontation marked the end of that established maroon community.[18]

Much of Joe's life remains a mystery besides the path blazed in newspaper reports of his deeds. Joe's scars described in the governor's proclamation give evidence of a life filled with trauma, resistance, and violence. He did strike fear in a wide swath of coastal and central South Carolina. In the petition by a number of residents for the rewarding of freedom for Royal, whose assistance brought Joe's death, it was stated "a series of villainy heretofore unparalleled in this state, had become a terror to a number of the petitioners with others." Joe had directly challenged the institution of slavery in the boldest manner, and his actions reflected Vesey's plot. Other famous runaway slaves in their confrontation of slavery have become historical heroes. Harriet Tubman, who carried a pistol with her in bringing other slaves to freedom from the South, was not alone in this practice. William Still, who collected and published stories about slaves making their way to freedom, noted that many were armed and prepared to use their weapons. Frederick Douglass, who physically battled an overseer whose intent was to bind and whip him, later asserted, "This battle with Mr. Covey was the turning-point in my career as a slave... I did not hesitate to let it be known of me, that the white man who expected to succeed in whipping, must also succeed in killing me."[19]

Joe's death occurred within five miles of the grave of a famous South Carolina hero, Francis Marion. What a contrast in how these two men were viewed by those in power: infamous villain versus enduring hero. From another viewpoint, one may see their similarities; both were intimate with the woods and wetlands, and able to exploit the environment for survival and stealth. They both fought tyrannical systems and conditions they refused to accept and risked their lives in their resistance.

· CHAPTER ·

WOMEN OF HAMPTON

Letter from Eliza Lucas Pinckney, from Hampton Plantation, to her youngest son, Major Thomas Pinckney, at camp at Parker's Ferry, on May 17, 1779.

> *Harriott will write to you now if possible. She is happy in being able to assist her friends at this time. She sent for Sally and the children upon the first appearance of Danger, and we were happy when we got them with us. Mrs. Middleton, Lady Mary, Mrs. Edward Rutledge, Mrs. Charles Drayton, Mrs. Ralph Izard and Mrs. Mathewes are now here with all their little ones. Mrs. D. Huger, Mrs W. H. Drayton and children with Miss Elliott and Miss Hyrne left us this morning to go to Peedee.*[1]

What was the "Danger" that brought these women to Hampton Plantation on the South Santee River, miles north of Charleston, in the spring of 1779?

In the fall of 1778 British forces landed in Georgia and captured Savannah, the beginning of their southern strategy. From that base the British began attacks between Savannah and Charleston, and a force led by General Augustine Prevost generated a path of destruction between Savannah and Charleston. Eliza Pinckney's youngest son, Thomas, detailed his losses at his Ashepoo River plantation in a letter dated May 17, 1779.

> A North Carolina soldier was five days sick at my house at Ashepoo, and was there when the enemy came. He reports that they took with them nineteen Negroes, among whom were Betty, Prince, Chance, and all the hardy Boys – They left the sick women, and the young children, and about five fellows who are now perfectly free and live on the best produce of the plantation. They took with them all the best Horses they could find, burnt the dwelling House and books, destroyed all the furniture, china, etc, killed the sheep and poultry and drank the liquors.

The British had visited Eliza Pinckney's home plantation Belmont just a few miles out of Charleston on the Cooper River and "destroyed every thing in the house, but took none of the negroes." These losses on Pinckney estates were just the beginning of devastation in the Lowcountry for those aligning with the Revolution. The plantations south of Charleston, and the estates on the Ashley and Cooper Rivers, were now in the bullseye. For these women, the lives of their husbands and other family members were in jeopardy, in battle, and in the consequences of imprisonment.[2]

Suspense and apprehension prevailed for months. Eliza's daughter Harriott, when alone at Hampton with her two young children, wrote her mother on December 30, 1778, to express her anxieties, including "the apprehension of the Enemy's coming here." One of Eliza's biographers, family member Harriott Horry Ravenel, empathized with Harriott's plight, "A young woman with one little boy and a baby…alone on a plantation with no white man, and listening to the tales which the negroes gather and spread with amazing rapidity. . ."[3]

The Hampton mansion. A number of generations of Horrys and Rutledges lived in the Hampton house before the property was sold to the state in 1971.

So who were these women gathering at Hampton? (Please note brief bios of the men in Notes.)

Sally was Sarah (Middleton) Pinckney (1756–1784), the youngest daughter of Henry Middleton (1717–1784) and Mary B. Williams (1721–1761). Sally had two young daughters with her, and would bear a son in September.[4] She was the wife of Eliza's oldest son, Charles Cotesworth Pinckney (1746–1825).[5] Sally was in the company of two sisters, and a sister-in-law.

Mrs. Middleton was Esther Mary (Izard) Middleton (1747–1814), Sally's sister-in-law, and the daughter of Walter Izard and Elizabeth Gibbes. Mary, known as Polly, was the wife of Sally's oldest brother, Arthur M. Middleton (1742–1787).[6]

Mrs. Edward Rutledge was Sally's sister, Henrietta (Middleton) Rutledge (1750–1792). She was the wife of Edward Rutledge (1749–1800).[7]

Mrs. Charles Drayton was Hester (Middleton) Drayton (1754–1789), the third Middleton sister. She was the wife of Charles Drayton Sr. (1743–1822).[8]

Lady Mary was Lady Mary (Mackenzie) Middleton (1730–1788), the stepmother of the three Middleton sisters, and the daughter of Archibald Mackenzie, the third Earl of Cromartie in Scotland, the source of her hereditary title. She was the fourth wife of Henry Middleton (1717–1784),[9] and was widowed for the fourth time at his death in 1784.

Mrs. Ralph Izard was Alice (DeLancey) Izard (1745–1832), niece of Governor DeLancey of New York, and wife of Ralph Izard (1742–1804).[10]

Mrs. Mathewes was Mary (Wragg) Mathews (1745–1799), and wife of John Mathews (1744–1802).[11]

Mrs. D. Huger was Sabina (Elliott) Huger (1758–1799), and wife of Daniel Huger (1741–1799).[12]

Mrs. W. H. Drayton was Dorothy (Golightly) Drayton (1747–1780), wife of William Henry Drayton (1742–1779).[13]

One wife was missing: Thomas Pinckney's (1750–1828);[14] there was no Mrs. T. Pinckney yet. It would not be long before he returned from his regiment camp to marry his neighbor from Fairfield Plantation, just downriver from Hampton, Elizabeth "Betsy" Motte (1757–1794), daughter of Jacob Motte II and Rebecca (Brewton) Motte. The marriage took place on July 22, 1779, within two months of the May 17th letter from his mother; their first child, Thomas, was born in the following year.[15]

The home of Harriott that provided refuge for all these women and many children was Hampton Plantation, located on the South Santee River in St. James

Santee Parish. "Harriott" was Harriott Pinckney Horry (1748–1830), daughter of Charles Pinckney and Eliza Lucas Pinckney, and sister of Charles Cotesworth and Thomas Pinckney. She was the wife of Daniel Huger Horry (1735–1785), who had acquired Hampton Plantation by inheritance from his father. Harriott married the widowed Horry in 1768, and bore two children: Daniel Horry (1769–1828) and Harriott Pinckney (Horry) Rutledge (1770–1858). Like her mother Eliza, Harriott did not marry again after the death of her husband in 1785.[16]

This group of women had sought shelter north of Charleston as a refuge from the British invasion. It was a roll call of the Lowcountry white elite, a group with considerable wealth and political power: Pinckney, Middleton, Rutledge, Drayton, Izard, Gibbes, Elliott, Wragg, Bull, Huger, Horry, Motte, and Brewton. Their husbands had sided with the Revolutionary cause, and the men's potential capture by the British could mean trial for treason and death by hanging. There were multiple family and social connections in this group. John Drayton Sr., after the death of his second wife, Charlotta (Bull) Drayton, shipped off his two young sons to school in England. They were under the care of Eliza Pinckney and her husband, Charles Pinckney (1699–1758), and accompanied the Pinckneys' three children: Charles Cotesworth, Thomas, and Harriott. During this time, John Drayton Sr.'s brother, Thomas Drayton III, married Lady Mary Mackenzie (her second marriage). Lady Mary's marriage (her fourth) to Henry Middleton in 1776 would equal John Drayton Sr.'s fourth marriage in 1775 to a seventeen-year-old daughter of a neighbor. It is not hard to find in these relationships examples of mercenary marriages.[17]

Almost a year after the writing of Eliza's letter, General Benjamin Lincoln surrendered Charleston to the British. The marriages of these women, who retreated to Hampton, connected them to the Revolution by their husbands, but there would be a fracturing of this alliance as some of the men decided to accept "protection," renewing their allegiance to the King, and therefore protecting themselves and their properties. These men and their families would face significant consequences in the aftermath of the eventual victory of the revolutionaries.

The case of Harriott Pinckney Horry and her family is one example of the reverberations of protection. When Charleston fell, Harriott's brother, Charles Cotesworth Pinckney, and her husband Daniel, were both serving as officers. The British imprisoned Pinckney at Snee Farm Plantation; Horry accepted protection, a decision shielding his properties from confiscation. He did not join the British cause but instead returned to Hampton, and subsequently took his son Daniel to England for his education. Harriott stayed at Hampton to manage the properties, and provided ongoing support for the Revolutionary cause. These efforts made a difference after hostilities ended, when the S.C. General Assembly did not confiscate but instead amerced the Horry properties. In fact, Harriott petitioned the Assembly for reimbursement of supplies she gave to Francis Marion's forces during the war. Her husband returned in 1782, and died in 1785. Her son did not return to claim his inheritance, instead marrying and living in France for the rest of his life. He also changed his name to Charles Lucas Pinckney Horry, and speculation about this decision includes possible shame about his father's actions during the war. Her daughter, Harriott, would marry the son of John Rutledge, Frederick, and they would have eight children and make Hampton their residence. Harriott, the mother, was left to manage the Horry plantations for the rest of her life, and she outlived her son.[18]

Eliza Lucas Pinckney (1722–1793) achieved a level of fame almost unparalleled relative to other women in the Revolutionary era. There are numerous biographies of her life, by scholars, a great-great-granddaughter, and an author writing for youth readers. Her story became prominent in school textbooks. George Washington requested to be a pallbearer when she passed away. The preservation and access to her extensive correspondence has enhanced her legacy, giving us insight into this remarkable woman.[19]

Eliza was born in Antigua, daughter of Anne Mildrum and George Lucas, a lieutenant governor of the island colony and a major in the British army. After her family moved to South Carolina and the family plantation Wappoo, she began to manage the plantation enterprise at age sixteen for her absent father. Her role in the cultivation of indigo at Wappoo has credited her in many accounts for introducing indigo in Carolina, but historians have recognized that she received help from several sources. She did produce a viable crop that contributed to indigo's growth as a cash crop in the colony. In 1744 she married the widowed Charles Pinckney (1699–1758). They moved to his plantation Belmont on the Cooper River, and together they had three children surviving to adulthood: Charles Cotesworth, Harriet, and Thomas. In 1753 the family moved to England where the children received their education. Charles, Eliza, and Harriott returned to South Carolina in 1758. After the death of her husband that year, Eliza was once again a plantation manager, revisiting the role of her teenage years. A main focus for Eliza was the education and nurturing of her children; her attentions to her two sons earned her the label "republican mother." This role of republican motherhood allowed women to participate in the greater political arena through the moral education of their children. Eliza at various times visited and lived at Hampton with her daughter, including during George Washington's visit in 1791. In 1793, she sought treatment for breast cancer in Philadelphia, and passed away there.[20]

The many letters from Eliza's youth illustrate an exceptional young woman. She expressed a combination of daily discipline, wit, piety, initiative, self-improvement, and virtue. In one letter, she commended a friend and frequent correspondent, Miss Bartlett, on her efforts to not oversleep, and went on to advocate for rising early. Besides waking daily at 5:00 a.m. (despite a neighbor's warning about premature aging) for study, she also spent time teaching her younger sister and "two black girls" to read. One of her "schemes" was training these girls to become "school mistres's for the rest of the Negroe children." As she described a recent endeavor to plant a fig orchard, she reflected on how Bartlett's uncle, Charles Pinckney (her future husband), kidded her about having "a fertile brain at scheming." As a retort, she asserted "I only confirm him in his opinion; but I own I love the vegitable world extremly." She referenced Pinckney's comments about her again in another letter to Bartlett: "Tell the little Visionary…come to town and partake of some of the amusements suitable to her time of life." Her precociousness was evident in her self-study of the law, and she wrote wills for some of her less wealthy neighbors.[21]

In a longer letter to her brother George, Eliza espoused her Christian faith and implored him to do the same. There were many examples in her letters of the importance of virtue, and in the nurturing of her children, she focused on imparting these values. She mentioned in a letter to Becky Izard: "I am convinced that Virtue is the only solid foundation for happiness and if we can obtain that my friend in all its amiable Branches we are secure of it married or Single or whether Fortune smiles or Frowns." Her listing of moral guidelines had God and family at the apex. One letter stood out, written to her fifteen-year-old son Charles Cotesworth Pinckney during his education in England. "From you, my dear Child, I hope better things, for though you are young, you must know the welfare of a whole family depends in a great measure on the progress you make in moral Virtue, Religion, and learning, and I don't doubt but the Almighty will give you grace and enable you to answer all our hopes, if you do your part." In a 1780 letter to her other son, Thomas, Eliza poured out her anguish after learning about his imprisonment by the British at Camden, and his serious injury (compound leg fracture). She expressed her own "anxiety and melancholy apprehensions," and asked, "Gracious God support me in this hour of distress!"[22]

The interpretation of Eliza's life has changed over the years. In the early nineteenth century the historian David Ramsay placed her life in a nationalistic light as a Revolutionary patriot, concluding that her indigo accomplishments contributed to the colony's economy and the future possibilities of an independent country. Her great-great-granddaughter, Harriott Horry Ravenel, also casts Eliza in an 1896 biography as heroic and a prime example of republican womanhood, her life identified with the birth of the nation. Scholars have viewed

Eliza as "deputy daughter" when she managed her father's three Lowcountry plantations. During her marriage she would be a deputy for her husband, and later for her children. She was also a kin specialist, a builder of family and social networks. This network grew considerably after her marriage and the marriage of her children; Eliza's letter of May 1779 listing the gathered women at Hampton is a case in point. Her daughter Harriott assumed the role of deputy mother in the management of the Horry properties due to her son's residence in France, and as a deputy sister for her brothers as they pursued their legal and political careers. After Eliza's death in 1793, her daughter became the matriarch of the family, and continued in the role of plantation manager for thirty-seven more years. Both mother and daughter lived complex lives that eclipsed gender norms.[23]

Despite their stretching of traditional gender roles, barriers still existed. They did not have access to the same education their male siblings enjoyed. When Eliza's indigo cultivation efforts were published in the *South Carolina Gazette*, the author given credit was her husband, Charles Pinckney. Even the memorial plaque in Philadelphia's St. Peter's graveyard displays a gender bias.

> In an unmarked grave
> Lie the remains of
> Eliza Lucas Pinckney
> Of South Carolina
> 1723–1793
> She was the mother of
> Charles Cotesworth Pinckney
> And Thomas Pinckney
> Patriots, soldiers, diplomats
> Erected by Eliza Lucas Chapter,
> Colonial Daughters of the 17th century

Her main legacy, according to the memorial, was her role as mother of her two famous sons. And no mention is made of her daughter, Harriott Pinckney Horry, and her achievements. Granted, the bronze plaque limited the amount of text, but still it displays historic biases.[24]

Eliza and Harriott were women of the white planter elite and were slaveholders. There does not appear to be evidence in their writings of any opposition to the institution of slavery. Their voices are well preserved by their correspondence and journals, and accessible through published works and digital access. The voices of the enslaved women of Hampton are hidden; there are no extant letters or other written documents. There is no work such as *Incidents in the Life of a Slave Girl* by Harriet Jacobs to inform us about the world of the slave community of Hampton, a predominately oral culture. The voices of Pinckney and Horry overwhelm the stories of Hampton's enslaved women, their stories only accessed by different means.

The Hampton enslaved community contained many people. In the inventory of the estate of Daniel Horry in 1786, a total of 306 slaves were listed on his four Santee Delta plantations: Hampton, Wambaw, Laurel Hill, and Jack Bluff. The appraised value of these enslaved African Americans in this 1786 inventory was £15,269. Hampton was the most developed of these plantations; the three others mainly contained lands for crop cultivation. Hampton would have the majority of the 306 slaves, estimated at 100 to 150 during this time. A range of appraised values appeared with the names, with a high of £120 for Big Patty, and a number of women listed with the appraisal of £1 (Hannah, Old Chloe) suggested this low value was due to old age and/or disability. Perhaps Big Patty was a valued head cook or a trusted servant.[25]

Enslaved women functioned in a number of roles at Hampton during this period. Cooks were critical to the running of this large plantation; there would also have been kitchen gardeners. Other specialized jobs included sewing and clothes-making, nursing babies, cleaning, and taking care of certain members of the household as assigned servants. Most of Hampton's enslaved women were field hands, both working on upland crops like corn, and in the rice fields. We can get some idea of the distribution of jobs on Hampton in comparison to another rice plantation in the Waccamaw Neck area, Hagley Plantation. Of 86 total individuals in that Hagley slave community, the breakdown of the 47 women follows: prime hands (21), full hands (2), half hands (11), quarter hands (1), nurses (2), midwives (1), seamstresses (1), house cooks (3), children's cooks (1), overseer's cooks (1), house servants (2), and overseer's girls (1). With the task system in place, women would devote the remainder of their day to their own needs, such as tending family garden plots.[26]

One way to access the lives of the enslaved African American community is through archaeology. In response to the civil rights movement in the late 1960s, archaeologists began to seek sites to explore colonial African America. These efforts have continued to grow with the recognition that the enslaved had left "stories in the ground." Both private and public lands in the Lowcountry have received archaeological treatment to access these stories, including Drayton Hall and the Charles Pinckney National Historic Site. Hampton Plantation State

Historic Site has been an ongoing location for the study of African American life in the Lowcountry.[27]

Archaeologists documented investigations at Hampton Plantation in 1979 and 1980. More recent work looked at a settlement area to the west of the existing plantation house. In 2010, the foundation of a house and associated artifacts, particularly the large number of colonoware sherds, suggested the location of a slave dwelling. These findings helped to inspire the development of the Hampton Community Archaeology Project. Beyond the archaeological investigations, begun in March 2013, a goal of the project was to educate and engage park visitors, student groups, and the local community, particularly descendant communities. Archaeologists included volunteers in the fieldwork.[28]

The artifacts recovered gave some insight into the enslaved men and women living here. The project report's author carefully identified that while some of the artifacts could be related to women, such as a thimble, buttons, and other sewing items, there was evidence at Hampton of men working as tailors. A colonoware teapot invited speculation about its use for brewing teas with local plants, and perhaps for medicinal purposes. Other items, such as beads, glass items, and a pierced coin, had adornment purposes. Archaeologists recovered artifacts associated with activities: smoothing stones and shell scrapers for pottery making, and a spoon handle often used in sweetgrass basket making.[29]

Site of slave dwelling. A multi-year community archaeology project located and excavated the remains of a slave dwelling at Hampton Plantation State Historic Site.

While the lives of enslaved African American women are more difficult to access due to the stated reasons above, even more hidden are the lives of Native American women. Archaeologists have not yet identified the location of King Jeremy's plantation. King Jeremy was known as the leader of a coastal Indian tribe, the Sewees. Through artifacts recovered by archaeology at Hampton, we know there was Native American occupation here from the Archaic to the Mississippian period. Intact features may still be present beneath the surface. We also know of other Santee planters who owned Indian slaves in this period, and some Hampton slaves might have been of indigenous origin. Daniel Huger of the nearby Watahan and North Point plantations in a memoir noted having "slaves, Negroes as well as Indians."[30]

While there were probably other angels associated with Hampton Plantation, one woman named Sue Alston became known as the "Guardian Angel of Hampton." Affectionately known by family as "Ma Dueg," she was a renowned resident and employee, working for over seventy years for the Rutledge family.

It is not an overstatement to describe Alston as legendary. According to her obituary, she was born in Germanville (also known as Germantown) in 1873, and passed away in December 1983, at age 110. Alston had a remarkable longevity and well-lived life. She was the daughter of Lewis and Abbie Brown Collington, whom she described as "Lucas people," probably owned by the Lucas family before emancipation at Wambaw Plantation.[31]

When Archibald Rutledge returned to Hampton Plantation after inheriting the properties from his father, he sought to renovate the old (circa 1740) mansion. He recognized Collington as a very talented builder with many skills, and "kind of a genius." Rutledge and Collington worked closely together, but Rutledge deferred completely to Collington's problem solving abilities, who often found ingenious solutions to the renovation challenges.[32]

Sue Alston drew the attention of several presidents: President Reagan, whose birthday also falls on February 6, and President Nixon on her 100th birthday. She also received a postcard from President Ford on her birthday in 1976. In fact, her life spanned the terms of twenty-two presidents.[33]

Gerald Alston, one of Alston's extended family, got to know her in his youth in the Germanville community where they both lived. He, along with a friend and cousin, would visit her home. She would give them treats, and they would rake her yard and bring in firewood. He used Ma Dueg as her honorific name.

Henrietta Smalls, another member of the Germanville community, was Alston's godchild. When she was growing up, her parents would take her over to Alston's to spend the night. She recalled that Sue Alston was a real "church lady," attending regularly at Howard AME church in Germanville. She described her as the mother of the community. When asked about Alston's focus on manners, Smalls related a saying of hers: "Manners, manners, she'd always say manners would take [you] where nothing else, where money can't carry you." Smalls recalled another teaching of Alston's often imparted to younger people: "Have manners, and be nice to people. We're all people. We're all God's children. God loves us all." In Alston's later years, Smalls mentioned how she and other members of the community had reached out to help her. Alston declined Smalls' offers to wash her hair or clothes. She wanted to stay independent.[34]

Jim Fulcher also remembered Sue Alston. Fulcher, a family practitioner, was Alston's doctor in her later years, and first saw her as a patient when she was visually impaired due to cataracts. He sent her to have the cataracts removed, and during her next visit to his office, she exclaimed (seeing him for the first time): "Thank the Lord! The baby doctor done come!" (Fulcher was in his forties at the time.)

He also recalled going with his wife, Patty, and four-year-old daughter Allie to visit Alston at her cottage at Hampton. At one point, Allie walked over to the sitting Alston and placed her small hand on her lap. Alston placed her hand over Allie's, and Allie added her other hand over Alston's. The Fulchers remembered it as a most sweet moment in the presence of "a beautiful person." When asked if Alston's longevity was the result of her genes, Fulcher suggested an important contributing factor: her spirituality. He took care of another female African American centenarian who also had a strong faith. He asserted that God's spirit shone through in Alston.[35]

The voice of Archibald Rutledge has carried long and far through his many writings, and he helped to establish Hampton Plantation as a prominent place in the history of the Lowcountry. He was the employer of Sue Alston for many years. He recognized her outstanding qualities, and one story he shared in his book *God's Children* captures her deep faith and spirituality.

> *She has raised all the orphans and the illegitimates. To be down and out is to have Sue take you into her home and care for you. Since her home for many years has really been overworked by her generosity, and was caving in, I built for her in my own yard a humble but immaculate cottage. She had hardly moved in before she took in with her the most disreputable Negro woman in the whole country, to nurse back to health and virtue. But it jarred me. "Sue," I protested,*

"How could you take that creature into your new home?" Looking at me with deep eyes that saw something beyond the range of my vision, she answered gently, "Jesus would."[36]

In a 1976 interview, Alston received the attention of the journalist and author John Egerton, whose extensive writing career covered the civil rights movement and Southern culture. In the interview, Alston mentioned how her father and mother were "Lucas people"; she related how her father had come over from Wambaw Plantation, and that her mother had lived on Murphy Island. Alston married "the best man at Hampton, Prince Alston," and together they had five children. She worked for the Rutledges as a cook, but also "took care of the tourists." She quoted her grandmother, Betty, when talking about the Hampton slaves being set free by the Yankees: "You see, they were free to a certain extent, see, they wasn't all together turned loose, you see. The Yankee bust the old slavery chain, but he didn't take the rope 'way." In the interview, she kept emphasizing the importance of manners and principles. She asserted, "Well, if I respect my white people and know to treat them and they know how to treat me, I wouldn't have to ask how I'm going to treat that gentleman." In regards to the changes of modern times, Alston reflected, "Some morning I get up and want to go right back to old times. My old life that I come from…In my time you

Chimney remains of Prince and Sue Alston's house, Hampton Plantation State Historic Site.

had your hoe your hatchet your saw you make everything you need…I don't care you can have money stacked up high, they ain't going to live how my life was. I could praise God and I could have manners to my white people. Praise the Lord." When asked if she would ever see Hampton return to "the old days," Alston didn't think so, stating, "I'll be in Hampton anyhow, but I'll be laying down, but my spirit will be there, yes Lord."[37]

There is a strong echo in Alston's life to that of Eliza Lucas Pinckney. After their husbands passed away, neither Pinckney nor Alston remarried. Both of these women had strong principals guiding their choices. Their moral foundations were religious faith, piety, and virtue. They became matriarchs of their families, and leaders in their communities. The examples of their lives provide enduring legacies.

• CHAPTER •
6

TALE OF THE TWO GREAT CANOEISTS

One sailed north, the other rowed south, traveling on opposing journeys. The craft were likewise different, though both voyagers called their vessel "canoe": one propelled by oars, the other by sails. One was "factory" built on the Hudson River, the other crafted from the remains of a wooden ship and native woods of the Brazilian coast. The fourteen-foot paper canoe *Maria Theresa* carried only Nathaniel Holmes Bishop; the thirty-five-foot *Liberdade* was temporary home to Joshua Slocum, his wife and two children. Fourteen years separated these epic voyages by Bishop and Slocum, and their courses finally crossed on the South Carolina coast as they sought shelter overnight on Murphy Island.

Murphy Island has always been off the beaten path. This isolation prevails despite its incredible natural beauty: unspoiled beaches, ridges of maritime forest, vast wetlands, and the waters of the Atlantic Ocean, the South Santee River, and numerous impoundments and tidal creeks. It is a watery world—less than 10 percent of its 7,927 acres are upland—a reality contributing to the deaths of many enslaved people during the Great Gale of 1822 when the entire island was inundated by the storm surge. Looking beyond the island's natural splendor lies man's substantial impact: the transformation of the island's abundant marshland through the construction of dikes, water control devices, and canals into the fields and hydraulic works required for rice cultivation, an immense feat carried out by the enslaved labor force. Even at the zenith of the Rice Kingdom, the island was still incredibly isolated; the South Santee River's shallow outlet to the ocean was ill suited for commerce. Murphy Island during Reconstruction and afterward regressed even further into a backwater, and was a most unlikely place for visits from travelers, nevertheless two men on epic voyages.

As their journeys and craft differed, so too did the backgrounds of these two men. Though both "Yankees," Bishop came from a privileged upbringing in Medford, Massachusetts next to Boston, while Slocum grew up in poverty on a farm in Nova Scotia. Bishop received his education at the elite Lawrence Academy, while Slocum withdrew from school in the third grade to accompany his family in a move to Westport, and to labor in his father's boot shop after the farm's failure. Both men left these circumstances to begin adventuring in their teenage years. Bishop went on a solo one-thousand-mile walk across the South American continent from the La Plata River and over the Andes to Valparaiso; Slocum left home at sixteen and went to sea to start a maritime career. While the beginning of their adventures had different motivations, they both found a desire to chronicle their trips, and the reading public responded with interest.[1]

It was during the 1870s and 1880s that each of these "canoeists" set forth on voyages taking them through South Carolina. Their reception along the Lowcountry coast was generally positive in regard to their Yankee heritage. Bishop stopped on Murphy to seek shelter, while Slocum's visit coincided with his first landfall on the mainland. The island's former rice plantations were no longer in production, though residents still cultivated rice for their own tables. Bishop and Slocum came face-to-face with the poverty of Southern blacks and whites on this isolated barrier island, and documented their experiences in their respective books: *Voyage of the Paper Canoe* (Bishop), and *Voyage of the Liberdade* (Slocum).

We set off from McClellanville out of Jeremy Creek in a seventeen-foot canoe, headed for three days and two nights paddling to Murphy and Cedar Islands in January 2014. There was only one "great canoeist" aboard: Ian Sanchez, friend and accomplished paddler of canoes and kayaks. He had made a memorable kayak journey in 2008 from the upstate to the coast, documented in a SCETV production *Web of Water*. He assumed the seat of honor in the stern, and after observing my paddling skills helped me to utilize my core muscles for more efficient effort. The lesson was thoroughly utilized on the three-day journey.

Ian Sanchez, the engine in the stern of the canoe on a trip to Murphy and Cedar Islands in 2014.

It was a most inauspicious beginning to our trip. During the first hour paddling through a Cape Romain National Wildlife Refuge creek on our way to Murphy Island, I warmed up and shed a layer. I heard a "plink" in the deep creek, and realized my prescription glasses had gone to the bottom. I had no backups on board, and my role as navigator became more difficult, leading to an early wrong turn. We finally found our way out Alligator Creek to Cape Romain Harbor, and the shore of Murphy Island.

After our landing, we had time to explore the oceanfront, and I recalled a very hot 2008 walk where I crossed the creek historically dividing "Little" and "Big" Murphy Islands, which required wading through chest-deep waters. We had no intention of such a crossing on this cool January day. We returned to set up camp and prepare for what would be a night of rain, heavy at times. The surf noise grew louder in the night, and at dawn the reason was clear: small waves were breaking on the shore of our campsite.

We made a resolute launch in the rain of the early morning, pushing the canoe out until we jumped in and paddled hard to ascend the small waves, only taking one over our bow. Retracing our paddle up Alligator Creek against the tide, the grayness of the day was ubiquitous except when separate blotches of white and black (white pelicans and black cormorants) appeared on a point of Cape Island. We continued on around the southwestern end of Murphy to the Intracoastal

Waterway (ICW) in the increasing rain, and stopped off on a sandy bank to step up on the dike and peer into the island's interior.

My losses continued. My voice had disappeared from a cold, and upon stepping out of the canoe I experienced "canoe legs," requiring me to grab the canoe to avert landing in the water. Peering through the tall aquatic grasses, we observed vast wetlands stretching off to the east, an area appearing as huge and inscrutable as an African savannah. We left the ICW when we entered the continuation of Alligator Creek, and floated past the entrance to a major canal of the island, once equipped with gates. Entering the South Santee River, we paddled downriver along Murphy until we landed again at one of the island's ridges for a brief visit to the historic storm tower.

We utilized the last of the outgoing tide on our way to Cedar Island, and our camp on Cedar Point. Soon after our landing, we saw the first sun of the day, and proceeded to dry gear, set up camp, and wander. The clearing skies presented fine views to Cape Island, the lighthouse beyond to the south, and the other end of Cedar Island to the north. I recalled another hot day hiking Cedar Island's beach from end to end in 2012. It was a cakewalk compared to the long paddle and sail (five hours) that day from the South Island Ferry Landing to arrive at Cedar's northeast end, though the return sail required less than two hours. There was a pattern in the necessary challenges to arrive at these Santee Delta barrier islands.

The moon, accompanied by Jupiter, rose before sunset. The astronomical and atmospheric delights continued in the early morning when we launched before sunrise to work our way up the South Santee River. The agreed-on early start was necessary to make the Pole Yard Landing by noon. The moon and Jupiter set over Murphy as we entered a fog bank. This ethereal experience rewarded all the challenges of the journey, some of which lay ahead. The fog burned off prior to our finding the entrance to Pleasant Creek and then Sixmile Creek on our crossing to the North Santee River. As we expected, we encountered a stiff outgoing tide combined with strong river current, and any halt in paddling meant we would move backwards. So on this last leg we faced a relentless grind, paddling upstream toward our destination for one and a half hours. We made it to the landing by our deadline; my voice was completely gone. The minor discomforts and difficulties of this three-day canoe voyage gave me a limited idea of what Bishop's and Slocum's journeys entailed, and the life-threatening emergencies they faced.

Bishop began his great journey in 1874, rowing from Quebec to the Gulf of Mexico, a trip of twenty-five hundred miles. He started out with a heavy wooden boat and a rowing partner, but left both on the Hudson River when he switched to a lightweight (fifty-eight pound) canoe built by E. Waters & Sons, Paper Boat Builders, at Troy, N.Y. By the winter of 1874, the "paper-canoe captain" was traveling through the inland waterways of the Carolinas. All along the way, locals disparaged the perceived fragility of this craft made from laminated paper, including the hardy women and men of Ocracoke, NC, saying, "I reckon I wouldn't risk my life crossing a creek in her" and "That feller will make a coffin for hisself out of that yere gimcrack of an egg-shell."[2]

A storm delayed Bishop's crossing of the Santee River "which kept me a weary prisoner among the reeds of the rice marsh." He lay in the canoe all night, cramped and not able to build a fire. The next afternoon he pushed off into the rough waters, and successfully made the crossing. The storm raged anew, and he sought shelter at a cabin on stilts. Rebuffed by the black overseer of the plantation, another black man, Jacob Gilleu, gave him directions to Seba Gillings's place near Alligator Creek on Murphy Island. Gilleu did not comprehend when Bishop stated he was "a citizen of the United States," but understood when told that the United States was the land that Grant governed. Bishop rowed on and turning off of Alligator Creek, moved through an open tide-gate into a canal penetrating Murphy Island. He landed at a piece of higher ground from the marsh, where a dozen houses—"a negro hamlet"—existed along with the

Home of the alligator. Nathaniel Holmes Bishop rows his paper canoe on a southern waterway.

ruins of a rice mill. Bishop most likely found this isolated small community of freedmen on the southwest end of Settlement Ridge. Seba Gillings met Bishop, helped to put the canoe in a safe place, and took him to his house.

Gillings supervised the preparing of a meal for Bishop: his wife pounded the rice in a traditional mortar, and his son cooked bacon and eggs. Bishop ate alone at the table. After the table was cleared, he was in for a startling experience.

> *Then we gathered round the great, black-mouthed fireplace, and while the bright coals of live-oak spread a streak of light through the darkness, black men and black women stole into the room until everything from floor to ceiling, from door to chimney-place, seemed to be growing blacker and blacker, and I felt as black as my surroundings. The scant clothing of the men only half covered their shiny, ebony skins. The whole company preserved a dignified silence, which was occasionally broken by deep sighs coming from the women in reply to a half-whispered, "All de way from de norf in a paper canno – bless de Lord! Bless de Lord!"*[3]

The atmosphere became even more animated following the entrance of a young black skipper of a sloop after his passage from Charleston through Bulls Bay. He took center stage, and whipped up the onlookers in a religious frenzy before Seba Gillings dismissed all so "de Yankee-mans" could get some sleep. Bishop would spend the night in Gillings' closet. After leaving Murphy Island, Bishop recommended to other travelers through the southern waterways, "Keep away from cabins of all kinds, and you will by so doing travel with a light heart and even temper."[4]

Joshua Slocum's approach to Murphy Island came fourteen years later. Slocum as both owner and captain had lost his ship *Aquidneck* on the shoals of a bay along the Brazilian coast in December 1887. Still possessing his navigation gear and charts, and confidence as a mariner, he had decided to sail home in a small boat. Slocum crafted a vessel of his own design, appearing as a hybrid between a Cape Ann dory and a Japanese sampan. Though having limited resources, Slocum possessed a characteristic he later attributed to his father in a future book *Sailing Alone Around the World*, "My father was the sort of man who, if wrecked on a desolate island, would find his way home, if he had a jack-knife and could find a tree." Slocum completed the vessel and launched it on May 13, 1888, naming the "canoe" *Liberdade* (Liberty) in recognition of the emancipation of slaves in Brazil on that very day.[5]

The Slocums soon embarked on what would be a five-thousand-mile journey from Paranaqua, Brazil, and ending at Washington, D.C. They experienced a number of adventures, including sailing over a shoal with huge breaking waves

Joshua Slocum, wife, and two children aboard Liberdade. Courtesy of the New Bedford Whaling Museum.

in a gale at night, and receiving a keel-damaging bump from a fifty-foot whale. Fifty-three days after setting off from Brazil, they made the first sighting of the mainland of North America along Bulls Bay. They anchored the night of October 28, 1888, a couple of miles from shore, and with light winds finally made the mouth of the South Santee River two days later. They continued in the river to see if they could find inhabitants, and probably along the east end of Settlement Ridge spotted a farmhouse. This was the home of the Andersons, a poor white family consisting of husband, wife, and two sons. Their difficulties in making a living on this farm impressed Slocum, and soured his thoughts of returning to New England to attempt farming. He admired Anderson for his patience and unselfishness, noting that of all the unselfish men he had met along the coast, "Anderson the elder was surely the prince."

Anderson, who had fought for the Confederacy, was incredulous on hearing Slocum's account about the emanicipation of the enslaved Brazilians, especially the fact that it occurred without a war. Despite living a hard life, he was extremely generous in providing the Slocums with fresh food, prompting Slocum to relate that he had "received more garden stuff than I had ever seen offered for a dollar in any part of the world." Anderson shared his disbelief before Slocum departed, "And you came all the way from Brazil in that boat! Wife, she won't go to Georgetown in the batto that I built because it rares too much." Later on in North Carolina, sitting by a fire with thirty men at a fish camp, they all proclaimed that the story of Slocum's trip "was the greatest thing since the wah."[6]

Slocum continued north, eventually mooring at Washington, D.C. on December 27, 1888, and after a return home to the north, Slocum made a final sail in *Liberdade* to Washington, giving the craft to the Smithsonian Institution. He reflected at the end of his book, "With all its vicissitudes I still love a life on the broad, free ocean, never regretting the choice of my profession." These were prophetic words, as was his thought on Murphy that farming was not for him: his future farming effort on Martha's Vineyard failed. His voyage around the world on *Spray* at the turn of the century was the historic first solo circumnavigation, placing him in the pantheon of immortal navigators, and elevating *Sailing Alone Around the World* as perhaps the greatest sea story written.[7]

After Bishop's night on Murphy Island, he rowed on in his paper-canoe, eventually reaching the Gulf of Mexico. He too made the *Maria Theresa* a gift to the Smithsonian. Bishop's friends described the paper-canoe journey as "your wildest and most foolish undertaking." Not finished with adventuring, he chose a more comfortable craft for his next trip, a Barnegat Bay (New Jersey) sneak box, rowing the twenty-six hundred miles down the Ohio and Mississippi Rivers from Pittsburg to Florida. Unlike Slocum, he settled down with his wife on a New Jersey farm and cultivated cranberries. Bishop left a large bequest for his community's library. The end of his life diverged from Slocum's: the aging sailor and *Spray* both disappeared somewhere in the Atlantic, last seen leaving Martha's Vineyard in November 1908. Though the stories of these kindred spirits are different, together they left us with captivating historic snapshots of Murphy Island, and the enduring written legacies of their journeys.

· CHAPTER ·

SWIMMING THE SANTEE

Rivers allow for the transport of people and goods. They are also barriers for travelers when their paths reach these waters. The brownwater rivers of the east do not allow fording except in their upper reaches, and no bridges in the eighteenth and nineteenth centuries spanned these major waterways. The government authorized ferries for tolled passages. Out of necessity, people cobbled together rafts and "borrowed" boats. When the need arose individuals resorted to swimming.

The enslaved often responded to the subjugation of slavery by running away to freedom. For those runaways on foot, rivers presented significant obstacles in their flight. While the existence of records of runaways swimming the Santee is not known, the case of one man, Charles Ball, gives insight into this scenario. Ball had escaped twice from Georgia plantations and made his way north on foot. During his first flight, the Apalachee River in Georgia halted his progress. Having grown up as a slave in Maryland, he had developed confidence with deep water swimming in the Patuxent River. When encountering the Apalachee, he carried his gear on his shoulders and easily crossed this waterway. On looking back, he noticed a large alligator that had been tracking him. He later found a canoe to cross the Savannah River, but swam another river before pirating another canoe to cross a broad river (most likely the Congaree) to Columbia.[1]

Perhaps no other British officer struck more fear in the rebel forces than Banastre Tarleton. "Tarleton's Quarter" became synonymous with massacre. In 1780 this colonel led a mounted force that scoured the area between Charleston and the Santee River in order to pacify any rebel resistance. His pursuit of revolutionaries triggered several desperate swims.

Colonel William Washington, a younger cousin of George Washington, had arrived at the north side of the Santee with Virginia cavalry. They were on their way to aid General Lincoln in the defense of Charleston, but found the area between the Santee and Charleston under British occupation. They crossed the Santee at Lenud's Ferry, and surprised and captured a small British force along with many horses, though Colonel Elias Ball (Wambaw Elias) escaped on a horse. Ball rode to Strawberry Ferry and informed Tarleton, who immediately proceeded with his dragoons to Lenud's Ferry to intercept Washington's force. When they arrived at the ferry, they surprised the revolutionaries in the process of transporting the captured British soldiers across the Santee. The majority of Washington's troops were still on the south side. In short order the British rescued their captured troops, and overwhelmed the rebels. They killed or imprisoned most of the rebels, and took possession of all their horses and equipment. Colonel Washington and a few of his men swam across to safety, though others drowned.[2]

Tarleton figures in another swim, this time in the Santee Delta. Francis Marion had retreated from Georgetown after an aborted attack on the British. While Marion's men went on to their camp in the Santee swamp, he stopped at Hampton Plantation for a meal and an overnight stay. Harriott Pinckney Horry was the hostess, and alerted the slumbering Marion to the arrival of Tarleton and his British forces. She took him out the river side of the house, and implored him to swim to the other side of the creek to the island in the South Santee, now known as Hampton Island. The creek functions as a braided channel of the South Santee. Horry's daughter described his passage as "like a wild duck." He hid in the island's reeds throughout the night until the following day when he traveled up the river to reunite with his men. Tarleton did not come away empty-handed. He dined on the meal prepared for Marion and pilfered a Milton volume from the library.[3]

Almost two centuries later, necessity inspired a resident of the Santee Delta to make the swim of both rivers. Phil Wilkinson grew up in the Delta after his parents purchased and restored Hopsewee Plantation on the North Santee River. In his youth he joined a gator hunt, an activity legal in those days, with two men on a nighttime adventure in the Delta. With no success finding any alligators, they pulled their boat out and decided, in violation of wildlife regulations, to deer hunt instead. Heading down the road near Hampton Plantation towards Germantown, they shone lights to either side, trying to spotlight a deer. When blue lights appeared behind them, they knew they were in trouble. They jumped out of the car and took off on foot. Wilkinson was barefoot and managed to elude the pursuers, meeting up with one of his fellow hunters. They walked along the dirt road, but the game wardens again confronted them. One chased Wilkinson but he got away when his pursuer became entangled in the top of a downed pine tree.

Phil Wilkinson's motivation to run from the game wardens was his memory of escapees from chain gangs. During his childhood, there were several incidents of runaways in striped suits coming onto the family farm and asking for food and water. The family cook would provide for them, and after they had eaten, Wilkinson's mother would tell them she would wait an hour before calling the sheriff. Wilkinson had listened to their conversations, and that night during the chase, he went all out to escape, and avoid that fate.[4]

Wilkinson moved toward the river, knowing the area well from hunting. Avoiding thickets and other obstacles as well as he could and hoping to not have any close encounters with snakes, he swam the South Santee and walked barefoot across the land between the rivers. A final swim across the North Santee brought him to his home at Hopsewee.[5]

The Santee Gun Club came into existence in 1898, though it was an inauspicious beginning. The dues collected from its sixteen members in 1900 were not sufficient to pay its bills. By chance, a club member on a European steamer told the Boston resident E. D. Jordan about the club, and Jordan became an enthusiastic new member. On his first trip south to hunt at the club, he invited four other Bostonians along. To their dismay, no one greeted them in Georgetown. Their search led them to the wharf of C. L. Ford. They found the club's paddle wheel steamer *Gardenia*, but the captain and crew were absent. After rounding up the captain, they shoved off in the dark for the passage to the club in the

Santee Delta. As they came through Sixmile Creek into the South Santee River, the dog of one of the Bostonians, Gardner Perry, fell overboard. In the darkness, they considered the pet lost. When they arrived at the dock at Fairfield Plantation, which the club had leased for use of the house, Perry's dog was waiting for them. It had swum across the South Santee, and once on shore had followed the *Gardenia* upriver to Fairfield.[6]

Santee Gun Club members hunted ducks with the capable help of the African American guides who lived with their families on club lands. One of those families, the Garretts, lived on the old Blake's Plantation. George and Celia Garrett raised five boys and four girls. George was a trunk minder, and three of his boys became gun club guides. One of them, William Garrett, recalled a time in his childhood when he and his brother Moses were swimming off the pier in the South Santee. William and Moses decided to swim to a log, and when they got close realized it was a ten to twelve-foot alligator. They quietly swam back to the shore, and mentioned it to the game warden at the pier. The warden killed the alligator; William encouraged him to take it to the Garrett home, but the warden had other ideas.[7]

The Santee was not the most conducive environment for the average swimmer. In the days before the damming of the Santee, freshets, flood events, were times of great danger, and certainly a most perilous time for swimming. Archibald Rutledge ventured out in a canoe to see one of these events. He was frightened and sought safety in the lee of a cypress, where he observed wildlife being swept helplessly downstream. One notable exception was an otter swimming straight against the flow. "Of all this vast wild life community that I saw, he was the only one serenely composed, the only one I saw challenging that thunderous deluge." When confronted with a huge tree coming downstream broadside to the otter's course, the animal "with a nonchalance that was almost comical, when he was within a few yards of the burly old giant, humped his back, dived, and a few seconds later reappeared above the log, swimming as if dodging death in a raging tide were just fine sport."[8]

The South Santee River beyond a canal along the Santee Coastal Reserve.

· CHAPTER ·

They Changed the River

It was a remarkable event late in 1941, when the final spillway gates of the massive dam on the Santee were closed, and the lakes began filling. This taming of a major river of the east was the culmination of a two and a half-year New Deal project employing a huge budget and an immense work force. The damming would have significant impacts, intended and unintended, in South Carolina. The impoundment of the Santee would throttle the high level of freshwater discharge of the river, a consequence to be felt in the Santee Delta. As one Delta landowner expressed, "They changed the river."[1]

The damming of rivers in the Santee watershed began long before the large hydroelectric projects of the 1930s and 1940s. These earlier projects were small-scale dams on Santee tributaries mostly used to power gristmills, some built as early as the late eighteenth century. The textile industry and its mills triggered another wave of dams. Mill builders constructed a dam and impoundment on the Enoree River in Greenville County to power a mill in 1820, and in the 1870s a more substantial rock dam replaced the original. These and other small dams would have had little influence on the Santee Delta.

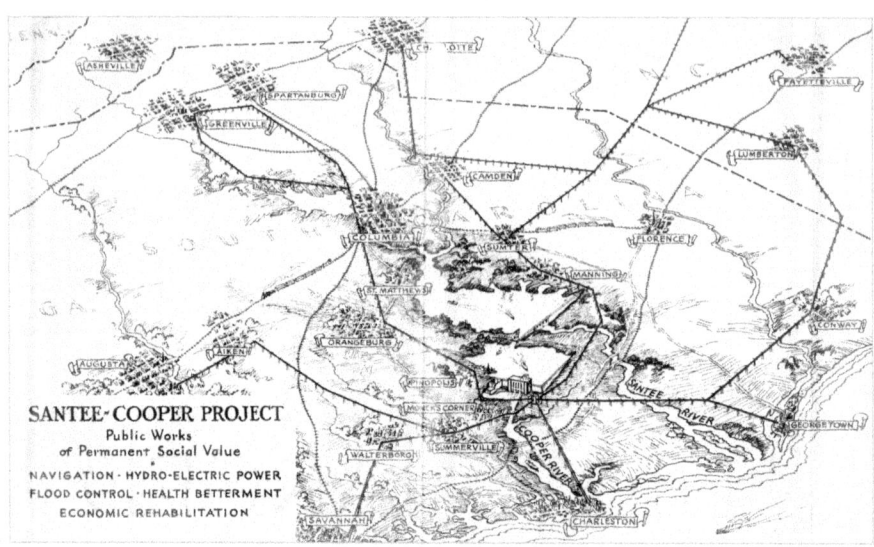

Illustrated map of the Santee-Cooper Project.

Other actions of man had a more noticeable impact downstream in the Delta. The lumber industry felled and removed trees in the Santee's floodplain. Additionally, farmers in the Piedmont cleared land to make way for the cultivation of cotton. As a result of these clearing efforts, increased flooding impacted the floodplain all the way to the coast after 1820.[2]

In his autobiographical *Home by the River,* Archibald Rutledge painted a vivid picture of a flooding event, a freshet of 1939, a few years before the impounding of the Santee River. He ventured out into the Delta initially to search for lost stock from his home at Hampton Plantation, but also to observe this flooded world and the impact on wildlife. "The immense and gloomy power of this deluge seemed to have the whole river country in its grasp. Majestic in its sinister power, and in places more than five miles wide, the Santee, carrying even at normal flow the largest body of water of any river in the East, ramped stormily to the sea, carrying with it thousands of swimmers, tons of flotsam—rafts of sedge, old pine and cypress logs—and whole years of debris from the mighty swamps to westward. The presence of all these obstructions in the water, and the speed at which they were being borne made swimming dangerous for anything. The wind and the waves were high; and the momentum of the flood had in it the irresistible power of an unleashed primitive force." This flood event was akin to an inland tsunami. Rutledge was frightened and sought safety in the lee of a cypress, observing wildlife being swept helplessly downstream. Reflecting on a freshet in early spring while paddling through the swamp forest of the Delta, he commented on the appearance of one species and avoided contact with any of the foliage, "almost every bush has, coiled upon it, or stretched prone on a low limb, or even festooning the top ten feet above the tide, a cottonmouth moccasin."[3]

In the first decade of the twentieth century, the first hydroelectric project of note in South Carolina was a collaborative effort between the tobacco baron James Buchanan Duke and the gynecologist and surgeon Dr. Walker Gill Wylie. They both had experimented with small-scale hydropower on their properties, and they imagined a much bigger project on the Catawba/Wateree River (the river changes names near Camden). Other projects followed on this same Santee tributary from the mountains to the fall line. In fact, in the next two decades this river became the most intensely developed for hydropower in the country. The initial project at Great Falls provided a seventy-one-foot head. In 1905 Duke and Wylie incorporated the Southern Power Company, later renamed the Duke Power Company.[4]

Damage from flooding was only one of the rationales for the large proposed hydroelectric projects of the 1930s. Poverty, unemployment, and literal starvation devastated the people of South Carolina during the Great Depression. The election of Franklin Delano Roosevelt promised for the nation and South Carolina relief and recovery. An influential senator from South Carolina, James F. Byrnes, became a great supporter of FDR's New Deal, and Charleston Mayor Burnett Maybank was also a solid backer of FDR.

There were national precedents for hydroelectric projects stimulating regional development: the Hoover, Bonneville, Grand Coulee, and Shasta Dams. Byrnes was a champion for several large hydropower projects. The first under consideration was the Buzzard Roost project on the Saluda River (also a Santee River tributary) in Greenwood County. The Public Works Administration (PWA) approved it in 1934, yet until a Supreme Court ruling on a similar case from Alabama would set precedent in 1938, the challenges from Duke Power stood. Officials contemplated a much bigger project from the 1920s with the concept of harnessing the seventy-five-foot gradient from the Santee River to the Cooper River. A New York engineering firm had already built Lake Murray on the Saluda River to the west of Columbia for hydroelectric power and to control water flow to the Santee-Cooper basin. The onset of the Great Depression stopped further Santee-Cooper progress in 1929.[5]

Initial efforts to restart this project could not proceed since PWA funds were not available for private companies. Senator Byrnes promoted the formation of a public service authority via a bill in the state legislature. This governmental agency proposed to improve navigation, generate and sell electricity, drain swamplands, and reforest the watershed. Some legislators opposed the bill, but it passed the state legislature. Challenges continued to the PWA funding of this project known as Santee-Cooper. This opposition included Harold Ickes, Secretary of the Interior and head of the PWA, who preferred smaller less expensive projects; Ickes also had concerns about the negative impact on the environment. Senator Byrnes, however, lobbied for the project's support since it would provide South Carolina a "fair share" of relief money and payback for his support of New Deal legislation.[6]

Opposition to the project surfaced from an environmental perspective. The nationally known and respected conservationist Jay Darling protested that the project would significantly upset the ecosystem in the Lowcountry. Darling was director of the Biological Survey (an earlier name for what would become the U.S. Fish and Wildlife Service), and he sent a letter to FDR opposing the project as a fiscal waste and an environmental disaster. A prominent ornithologist, Roger Tory Peterson, made a ten-day canoe and camping trip through the Santee swamp, and reported his concern that Santee-Cooper would destroy a huge pristine wilderness.[7]

The late 1930s and 1940s were very different times in terms of the protection of the environment. It was not until 1970 that the Nixon administration formed the Environmental Protection Agency and subsequently initiated mandatory Environmental Impact Assessments of projects with the potential to affect the environment. Congress passed The Endangered Species Act in 1973 as legislation to protect against the extinction of species. One notable species, the ivory-billed woodpecker, had historically lived in the Santee swamp, and in the 1930s the bird was listed as endangered. Between 1933 and 1935 an individual working on a wild turkey project observed the bird in the Santee River Swamp in Georgetown County. In May 1935 ornithologists from the Charleston Museum and the National Audubon Society confirmed sightings of the woodpecker in that section of the Santee near Wadmacon Creek just upstream from the Santee Delta. After the completion of Santee-Cooper, the sightings ended. Would the government have approved Santee-Cooper with a rigorous assessment of impacts to ecosystems throughout the Santee Swamp?[8]

Of several hunting clubs in the Santee Delta, the Santee Gun Club had the highest profile and began its opposition in 1930 through a letter writing campaign by the club's president, Philadelphia banker C. M. Clark, to the incumbent head of the Biological Survey, Paul G. Redington. Byrnes countered by hammering away at the "hunt club aristocrats," dismissing their concerns by suggesting their complaints were about having fewer ducks to shoot and losing value in their private power company securities. Maybank was on the ballot for governor of South Carolina, and he also took aim at the hunting elite's opposition to

Santee-Cooper. Other opposition included three private power companies who sued but eventually lost. Observers viewed the election of Maybank to governor in 1938 as a referendum on Santee-Cooper due to his advocacy of the project.[9]

So five years after the creation of the PWA, this agency allocated funds to start Santee-Cooper. The full SC budget for 1939 was just $12.5 million, while Santee-Cooper received $31 million (total for the grant-loan). The start of the massive project included property purchase, relocation of 901 families, and moving of 6,000 graves. Next came the clearing of both the 155-square mile Lake Marion and the 95-square-mile Lake Moultrie sites, 9,000 men in total accomplishing the work. Another 7,300 men excavated and built the canal, navigation lock, hydroelectric station, and 50 miles of dikes and dams. The project recruited workers from the relief rolls of every county in the state, the men residing in twenty-two camps, each accommodating 275 men. The Santee dam included an eight-mile-long earthen dam, a 3,400-foot spillway, and sixty-two massive gates used to spill excess water. In just over two and a half years, from land clearing to impounding of the Santee, Santee-Cooper was complete, and leaders touted the benefits. The employment of thousands of unemployed South Carolinians had a major impact on relief. The electricity generation stimulated

Edmund A. Cuthbert - in the great Santee River Swamp - south of Jordan's Cross Roads, Clarendon County, S.C. Clearing the swamp for Lake Marion.

industry expansion and rural electrification. In less than 25 years Santee-Cooper increased the number of farms with electrical power from 2 percent to 74 percent. Other benefits included a substantial reduction in malaria, and reduced danger to life and property from flooding. Santee-Cooper was certainly a blow to conservationists; the project's completion was a major loss of old growth forest in the South.[10]

One of the opponents of Santee-Cooper who wondered about its consequences was Archibald Rutledge, a resident of the Santee Delta, an outdoors writer, and the state's first poet laureate. His opposition through his writing prior to the project earned him a proposed punishment in the state legislature. A bill was introduced to censure him and strip him of his state recognition; the bill did not progress. In reflecting on the impact on wildlife, he initially remarked in his *Field and Stream* article "Dam Everything," "Of the wisdom of this project I have nothing to say. The thing is done." Rutledge restricted his observations to the fish of the Delta, noting the river was once fresh all the way to the mouth, but now the saltwater reached up ten to twelve miles from the ocean, due to the reduction in the river's flow. The saltwater flowed into smaller watercourses – creeks, canals, bays, channels – once the home of a number of species of freshwater fish. The fish inhabiting both fresh and salt in their life history—shad

Building of Santee River dam, part of the WPA construction of the Santee-Cooper Reservoirs.

and sturgeon—were now blocked in their access to historical spawning habitat far up the tributaries of the Santee. Rutledge wondered about the impact on freshwater bass with this major environmental change. He described the Santee as having been "polluted" by saltwater: "'Polluted' may not be the proper word; but, at any rate, a mighty change has been effected in the waters." The impact on both freshwater and saltwater fish remained to be seen.[11]

Another property owner in the Santee Delta, Pat Ferris on Cat Island, identified a different negative impact on his family's property. "It also cut the fresh water off from all the plantations on the Santee River, and salt water had a chemical effect on the banks. Banks that had had been there for years—that you can drive a pickaxe in, maybe an inch, if you swung it over your head—got soft and kind of gummy, and finally the banks just melted away." He stated that all the plantations sued Santee-Cooper for the damage to their properties, and since Cat Island was closer to the ocean than other properties, his family received just $6,000. The payment was enough to have a marine contractor build a new drivable dike around most of the property; 1,000 acres of old rice fields were lost in the process.[12]

Some of the other owners claiming damages to their properties were the Kinloch Gun Club (DuPont family), South Island Plantation (Tom Yawkey, owner of the Boston Red Sox), and most importantly the Santee Gun Club. This club had noticed a different form of damage to their earthen dikes. With the increased saltwater, fiddler crabs moved into the ecosystem and degraded dikes by their burrowing. The government rejected the club's initial effort to negotiate a settlement of $35,000. The club took matters into its own hands and rebuilt a good portion of the dike system. They presented the cost of that project and repair of earlier damage, $65,000, in another settlement attempt in 1953, but failed again. Eventually in 1960 the South Carolina Public Service Authority authorized a settlement of $35,000.[13]

During a public hearing in 1942 where property owners sought compensation for their damaged properties, Alan Johnstone, general counsel of the federal works agency, allowed that if there were damages the owners should be compensated. The response to owners challenging the level of flow down the Santee was another matter. The license from the Federal Power Commission required five hundred cubic feet per second to come down the Santee, and the property owners stated this amount was not enough. Johnstone stated: "We are now at war. I am advised by the chairman of the Federal Power Commission…that every kilowatt of power that can be generated by this development …is important to the safety and welfare of the United States. This is a war that will be decided upon the basis of production. That country will survive in the struggle that can outproduce its enemy. One of the principal means of production is electric energy." He went on to suggest it might be necessary to divert the entire flow. "It would be serious if anything should happen to interfere with the maximum use of this project in the defense of the United States and what it stands for in the world...Some of us may be required to give our lives 'without adequate compensation'. I suggest that no property rights would be of value should this country fall."[14]

Santee-Cooper was like no other dam project in the eastern U.S., yet the Santee River system and its tributaries had a history of many dam projects. In 2017, wildlife officials identified a total of sixty-six dams as obstructions to fish passage on the Santee and its tributaries. A measurable consequence of Santee-Cooper was the reduction in river flow. One volumetric measure of river flow is cubic meters per second (cms, or m^3s^{-1}). Prior to 1942, the average annual mean discharge was 525 m^3s^{-1}, and post diversion 74 m^3s^{-1}. An important variable in salinity levels was the impact of downstream flow seasonally and during dam release. The shellfish industry benefitted from the increased salinity in the Santee Delta; post diversion there was an increased productive environment for oysters and clams.[15]

Another unintended consequence of the diversion of the Santee's waters into the Cooper River was the increased sediment flow and siltation in Charleston Harbor. The project had projected that the initial diversion of the Santee flow into the Cooper would scour the Charleston Harbor and keep the channel deep; the reverse occurred. The port had a major impact on the Charleston area, the state's economy, and the viability of the Charleston Navy Base. The shoaling of the harbor threatened the port's future, and was so significant that a rediversion project was proposed in 1968. At one point Don Welch, chief executive of the State Ports Authority, took U.S. Senator Fritz Hollings to the proposed site in St. Stephen for a powerhouse that would redirect the waters. Without this project, Welch told Hollings, they would live to see corn planted in Charleston Harbor. In 1977 contractors implemented this project through the construction of a canal. The cost of the comprehensive rediversion project was $190 million. Forty-three years after the original diversion, the actual rediversion occurred in 1985. Officials estimated that prior to rediversion, ten million cubic yards of sediments from the Santee were collecting in the harbor annually, and after the rediversion only two million cubic yards required annual dredging to maintain the shipping channel. The mean annual discharge into the lower Santee was projected to increase from 74 to 428 m^3s^{-1}. This increased flow changed the salinity again, and as projected the changed waters damaged the oyster and clam industry in the Delta.[16]

Sediment deprivation along the coast near the Santee inlets was the corollary of the sediment deposition in Charleston Harbor as a result of Santee-Cooper. The beaches of Murphy and Cedar Islands have eroded more rapidly after the damming of the Santee. The sediment reduction out of the Santee has also accelerated the erosion of the northern Cape Romain islands, critical for loggerhead turtle nesting in the state.

Commercial fisherman Bob Baldwin from McClellanville had worked for years clamming and oystering in the Cape Romain area and vicinity. He was a first-person witness to the impact of the rediversion on the oysters:

> *After the rediversion the oysters got hit pretty hard, and they didn't come back... They died—from too much fresh water. They rediverted it in the summer of '85, and I had found a nice bed of oysters in the spring of '85, the last day of oyster season, I was just looking around on my way up the river and found a nice bed. And I said, OK, I've got a hot spot to come to next fall. And when they opened it up I went back there and dropped the dredge, and when I pulled it up it was like peanut shells, just nothing but rattles, everything was empty, they were all dead. All that water being fresh all summer long it killed them all. And the oysters died off way down the river, they, since it's been dry they've come back a little bit further up. The last two years the oysters have come back pretty well – we start having wet weather again I'm afraid they're going to die back again.* [17]

His projection of the effect of rain on increased freshwater flow and the impact on salinity was correct. The salinity changes created difficulties for plantation managers around the Delta utilizing impoundments to attract migratory waterfowl. They planted these "duck marshes" with a number of foods to attract the waterfowl. Rice had been an important food attraction for years, but the transition was made to other plant foods, including wild rice, wild celery, sago pondweed, and widgeon grass. Wildlife managers Kenny Williams at Kinloch Plantation and Phil Wilkinson at South Island Plantation managed salinity in their impoundments. The Santee Gun Club had these same challenges, and after its transfer to the state as the Santee Coastal Reserve, the South Carolina Department of Natural Resources (SCDNR) commissioned a study to look at salinity as it varied with changes in stream flow and tide stage after rediversion. The design of this study gave Santee Coastal the most accurate data in their impoundment management practices. By monitoring data from various tide gauges in the Delta, they were able to anticipate freshwater increases, and open and close water control structures as required.[18]

Another consequence not considered in the initial damming of the Santee was the blockage of anadromous fish from reaching their historical spawning grounds in the upper tributaries of the Santee. These fish, living in saltwater during adulthood and swimming into rivers to spawn, were abundant in the Santee Basin and included Atlantic sturgeon, shortnose sturgeon, Atlantic shad, hickory shad, and blueback herring. Another species of fish but catadromous (the reverse life cycle of anadromous) that historically had migrated in and out of the Santee was the American eel. Studies in 2007 and 2012 reported all of these species to have depleted population levels compared to historical levels, and one of the primary reasons for the decline was the barrier to spawning migrations and spawning habitat.[19]

As part of the Cooper River Rediversion Project, a fish passage facility, the St. Stephen fish lift, addressed the movement of anadromous fish to Lake Moultrie, Lake Marion, and beyond. A partnership of the U.S. Army Corps of Engineers with SCDNR, the United States Fish and Wildlife Service, and the National Marine Fisheries Service, collaborated on the design of this fish life project. In subsequent years blueback herring and American shad began to utilize the passage, and the numbers have annually averaged 400,000 American shad and 350,000 blueback herring. The lift received other modifications and repairs including the addition of wingwalls and gates in 1994, and an eel ramp in 2003.[20]

Despite the Rediversion Project, impediments continued to exist for anadromous fish. Plans for restoration of anadromous fish in the Santee Basin were formulated in 2001 and 2017. One of the agencies participating in the 2017 plan was the North Carolina Wildlife Resources Commission, since 28 percent of the Santee Basin area is in North Carolina. One important improvement resulting from the 2001 plan in fish passage above the lakes was the construction of a fish ladder at the Columbia Diversion Dam to allow American shad and blueback herring access to spawning habitat on the Broad River. The 2017 plan also outlined other proposals for fish passages on other upstream dams when fish populations triggered these assessments. One recommendation was an assessment of whether certain dams could be removed: Granby (Congaree River), Riverdale (Enoree River), and Whitney Mills (Lawson's Fork Creek, a tributary of the Pacolet River).[21]

Recent years have seen the successful removal of dams on rivers on both coasts, and the advocacy for more removals and overall river rehabilitation. While the dams on the small tributaries cited above might be removed in the future, it seems unrealistic that the damming of the Santee will ever be reversed. Oceanographer Björn Kjerfve, who studied the area in the 1970s before the actual rediversion, ventured an opinion on Santee-Cooper's impact on the Santee Delta estuary. He proposed an alternative for correcting the siltation problem: change the flow to the old Santee channel and release it through the Wilson dam. He did not agree with the Army Corps of Engineer's financial assessment that doing so, rather than their recommended rediversion canal project, would lose money due to the reduced hydroelectric generation. Kjerve reflected: "Large scale manipulations of river systems such as the lower Santee, is not an uncommon example of coastal management. ... *Intelligent* (his italics) coastal management, on the other hand, would have been to leave the Santee alone in the first place."[22]

· CHAPTER ·

Protecting the Delta

The Rice Kingdom began its decline after the Civil War, and the huge profits of the rice elite disappeared after emancipation. Commercial rice production continued in the Santee Delta only for the most financially secure plantations. The challenges confronted by planters after the Civil War included the destruction of rice culture infrastructure and neglect of rice fields during the war. The lack of capital precluded the repair of the infrastructure harmed by neglect and the destructive forces of hurricanes. A limited labor force and the higher cost of paid labor were other factors decreasing profitability. Competition with lower-priced rice came from the east (Asia), and from the west (southwest U.S.) later in the nineteenth century. The gradual withering of rice culture in the Lowcountry allowed the return of nature's dominion to many rice fields.[1]

The last decades of the nineteenth century saw the development of hunting preserves in other parts of the country for sportsmen. Property owners implemented management practices in these game areas for the cultivation of native food plants attractive to migratory waterfowl. These hunting clubs were recreation properties for the wealthy, and outside of the south industrial development created the opportunity to acquire wealth. The development of the shotgun around the turn of the century enabled waterfowlers much more accuracy in taking birds in flight, and stimulated the popularity of hunting.[2]

Birds had been longstanding nuisances to southern rice planters. On their annual migrations, bobolinks, also known as rice birds, fed on the plants in the spring, and in fall on the mature rice. Planters and their enslaved laborers went to great lengths to run off the birds. Migratory waterfowl also contributed to the destruction of the rice crop, and the Santee Delta's waters and wetlands were an important stop on the Atlantic Flyway. The Delta become a prime spot along the Carolina coast for northerners seeking winter hunting preserves due to the attraction of waterfowl to the rice crop, and the ongoing cultivation of rice. The decline in waterfowl numbers elsewhere generated this need for new hunting grounds.

The former rice plantations were in significant decline, and bankruptcy for the rice elite was common. The possibility of sale to wealthy Yankee sportsmen yielded an opportunity that many southern property owners could not turn down. Wealthy northern families such as the Yawkeys and DuPonts became landowners in the Delta. Owners established southern hunting clubs, where waterfowling became a main attraction for the gentleman membership.

One of the first clubs with northern members was the Annandale Club, formed in 1888. Originally located on Hobcaw Barony along Winyah Bay, the club later

Waterfowl on one of the managed impoundments in the Santee Delta Wildlife Management Area.

transitioned to Annandale Plantation on the North Santee River. The Santee Gun Club formed under the leadership of Hugh R. Garden in 1898 with thirteen charter members, and incorporated a larger collection of properties. In 1912 the DuPont Company purchased a number of properties on Kinloch Creek off the North Santee River and formed the Kinloch Gun Club. While not a club, Tom Yawkey's holdings on North and South Island were another northern sportsman's preserve, though a club of sorts was the beneficiary: the Boston Red Sox, the baseball "club" that Yawkey owned. Members of the Red Sox would visit the location. The legendary Ted Williams made his first visit to Yawkey's property after the end of his playing career. With Yawkey at the wheel of a Jeep, Williams in the front, and Phil Wilkinson in the back seat, they made a driving tour around South Island, looking at ducks and discussing fishing.[3]

The membership of the Santee Gun Club contained a majority northern contingent from New York, Philadelphia, and Boston. Besides the purchasing of lands to expand the club, they acquired *Gardenia*, a steam-powered boat equipped with a paddle wheel for use in transporting members to shooting properties, and as an early club house. In 1902 members contracted for the construction of a new club house on the mainland, rejecting a proposal for a site on Murphy Island. The club also employed a number of African Americans as guides and as household workers (cooks and maids). One of those guides, William Garrett, described the years during the Great Depression and through World War II. The employees, many who lived on the property, found the club well supplied. In the 1940s, the eighteen-year-old Garrett was glad to be employed when he went to work there. He began at $2.50 a week and reported being satisfied with that salary.[4]

The Yankee ownership and land development of these properties as waterfowl hunting preserves contributed to the next phase of the Delta's transformation. While some properties were able to maintain rice growth for duck food and the cultivated rice for baiting when it was legal, the end of rice cultivation led to the systematic propagation of duck food in the impoundments. Owners converted old rice fields by the planting of aquatic plants such as widgeon grass. For years plantation managers handled this work, but in the mid twentieth century the work became more specialized and the province of wildlife biologists. William Baldwin Jr. achieved renown for his work at the Santee Gun Club. Phil Wilkinson went to work for Tom Yawkey on his North and South Island properties, and Kenny Williams for the DuPonts and then Ted Turner at Kinloch. Peter Manigault recruited former South Carolina Wildlife Resources Department (now SCDNR) biologist Duff Holbrook for the management of his Delta properties. These wildlife biologists also recognized the importance of these managed wetlands for wading bird and shorebird habitat. Properties

Jimmy Singleton and an unidentified employee place duck decoys in the water near Kinloch Plantation.

with substantial resources such as the Santee Gun Club worked to rebuild dikes to protect these duck marshes, and used draglines and other heavy equipment rather than manual labor to mechanize the work.[5]

The value of the Santee Delta lands and the stewardship by their owners led to two extremely important donations to conservation and the state of South Carolina in the 1970s. In 1974 the Santee Gun Club disbanded and donated the 24,000 acres to The Nature Conservancy (TNC), which then transferred the properties to the state of South Carolina. This transaction had been in the works for some time, and represented the movement of TNC toward the development of state programs to inventory and protect significant properties. From the Santee Gun Club's gift, TNC held in their ownership the Washo Reserve, a 1,040-acre tract that included a freshwater cypress lake, cypress-gum forest, and the oldest continually active wading bird rookery in North America. Two years later, with the death of Tom Yawkey, a bequest in his will gave the 20,000 acres of his properties including North and South Islands and most of Cat Island to the state of South Carolina. Additionally the Yawkey Foundation set up a ten million dollar trust fund to support the operation of the lands now known as the Tom Yawkey Wildlife Center. These two gifts to the state were transformative, and had importance beyond South Carolina. Each donation was set up differently, though sharing the goal of wildlife management and conservation. While the Yawkey Wildlife Center had eliminated hunting on its lands, SCDNR's Santee Coastal Reserve continued some limited duck hunting each winter. The

The Santee Gun Clubhouse.

moniker "carpetbagger conservation" became a description of the process of the northern ownership of these properties and later donation to state and federal entities.[6]

I made my first trip to Murphy Island on December 27, 2006 on a public SCDNR duck hunt. Jim Westerhold of SCDNR arranged the trip, and I met him at 3:30 a.m. at the Sewee Outpost to follow him to Santee Coastal Reserve. At the check station there, the hunters signed in with the "patriarch" of the hunt, Bill Mace, the manager of Santee Coastal Reserve. Participation in this hunt was by a public drawing process, allowing only a small number of hunters and strict limits on the hunt. I talked to several hunters from Greenville, both Clemson graduates and professional golfers, who were looking forward to their first opportunity to hunt in this renowned place for ducks. Bill Mace conducted a meeting where he reviewed plans for the hunt, gave assignments for blinds, and reiterated limits (six ducks per hunter, twenty-five shell limit). Watches were synchronized; the legally established time for the commencement of shooting was 6:51 a.m.

At 5:00 a.m. we caravanned down to the landing on the South Santee River: Bill, Jim, several other DNR staff, about seventeen hunters, and myself. I stuck out like a sore thumb, as the only individual not sporting camouflage gear or carrying a shotgun. Three DNR watercraft would carry us over to Murphy Island. In the dark, the hunters bearing guns, bags of decoys, and packs walked single file down the dock as the DNR officials gave boat assignments. The whole event had the feel of a military operation as we headed out in the boats in the cover of darkness. The craft provided us some protection from the freezing temperature with a half cabin and windshield. The brilliance of stars punctuated a profound darkness, though a dim glow emanated from a Georgetown power plant in the distance. I chatted with one of the hunters, a teacher from Waccamaw High School, and he wondered if I was a newspaper reporter. The pair of golfers also pondered my reason for going along on the hunt, their speculations ranging from biologist to PETA member (joking, I think).

From the landing, we motored to the ICW, and then turned to the south. The vista was breathtaking, allowing views almost to the horizon. We arrived at the dock; one boat landed and disembarked at a time. Bill would deliver two pairs of hunters to their blinds, using a johnboat to navigate the canal system. I tagged along on this boat ride, while the others were taken to their respective blinds by pickup trucks and skiffs along the dikes. The boat ride started out to the north and turned through a maze of canals – I wondered how Bill could navigate this course in the pitch dark. Justin, a young DNR staffer, said that Bill could do these runs blindfolded.

We finally arrived at some high ground, which I later learned was the beginning of Settlement Ridge. Bill and staff pulled skiffs down to the water, Bill gave directions to their blinds, and the hunters embarked and paddled off. The two golfers didn't quite have the hang of paddling initially and veered off into the bank. Their course continued to be ragged, as if they were two campers learning to canoe for the first time. Bill was clearly miffed, but they were soon off in the right direction as we headed back.

A tremendous shooting star illuminated a large area of the night sky during our return course. Back at the dock, the other DNR staff members were waiting for us. They walked to the boats and prepared to head to the "office" until their return later in the morning. I inquired about where I could walk, and Bill directed me to the dike paralleling the ICW, away from the area of the hunt. I began the walk in pitch black to the south on the dike. The northwest wind was quite cold, so I used the movement to warm up. The walk was easy on the drivable and mowed dike. When I arrived at a water control structure, I heard the sounds of gunfire from the mainland and noted the time as 6:51. A night heron squawked and flew close by, disturbed by the shots. A few bends in the track took me away from the ICW and then back; there was no boat traffic this early.

Single shots soon rang out over Murphy, and the first slight lighting up of the sky appeared in the east. More birds became visible: a great blue heron, egrets, an eagle, and a large group of coots.

I planned to get back to the dock at nine o'clock when the others returned. As the light grew, more birds were taking flight. I continued the walk and speculated on the size of the old rice fields, having already covered a couple of miles on this dike. My path finally turned left, where Alligator Creek, the border between Santee Coastal Reserve and the Cape Romain National Wildlife Refuge, curved out from the ICW toward Cape Romain Harbor to the east. The Cape Romain lighthouse appeared in the distance across the marshes to the south.

On the return walk the huge scale of the rice fields became apparent in the daylight, and a series of canals laced through the wetlands. Bill Mace called the largest of these waterways rice barge canals, allowing the large plantation craft to navigate these intra-island passages. Bill had mentioned that this end of Murphy Island, originally known as Little Murphy Island, was infested with the invasive plant *Phragmites*, a plague also occurring to the south in Cape Romain National Wildlife Refuge. I reflected on the 1822 Great Gale, with its catastrophic right quadrant engulfing the island with storm surge and shrieking winds, killing so many.

I had shed a couple of layers prior to completing the walk back to the wharf. Soon the boat returned from the mainland and would ferry finished hunters back for breakfast. I opted to stay on the island and head over to the eastern side. I took advantage of a truck ride offered by Bill across the main dike to the east side of Murphy. The ride on top of the dike gave perspective on the rice fields and the blinds on either side. One pair of hunters had finished, and my driver Gilbert learned that they limited out (ten birds) and used all their shells. We continued to the beginning of the island's upland, and he dropped me off at the turnaround to meet back at 11, leaving me less than two hours for the walk. The forest road went both ways along this ridge, and I turned to the left to head northeast.

I walked along Tina Ridge on a mowed road framed by the maritime forest of live oaks and pines. Bill earlier remarked that Hurricane Hugo destroyed most of the mature pines, and the initial survivors died later. My goal was to make it to the ocean and/or the South Santee River. There were no biting insects, and the coolness of the morning made for exquisite walking. I shed another layer, keeping a steady pace to cover the maximum ground in the limited time. Fingers of wetlands intruded close to the ridge on either side; to the east beyond the wetland another smaller forested ridge stood. Upon a fork in the road, I took the option to the right toward the water, but soon found the road's end.

I struck off the beaten path, and some open sandy areas suggested old sand dunes. After a short bushwhack to the marsh, I climbed through some wax myrtles for a view. There was a short section of marsh separating me from the blue of the river and ocean junction; the sound of small waves lapped on the shoreline. Retracing my steps, I took the other direction at the fork. The road formed a crossing between extensive wetlands where ibises foraged. The path stretched out into the distance to the north, and I begrudgingly turned around.

On the return I speculated about a long loop hike around Murphy Island: starting on the south end of the island across from the north end of Cape Island, heading up the beach around into the South Santee River, finding a route to connect with the Tina Ridge road, following south until the road trails off, and picking the way through the forest back to the south end. I ran this idea by Bill Mace later, and he was pessimistic, stating there was "no future in it." One crucial bit of information I would need was whether there were creeks or canals creating barriers along the route.

I returned to the "T" of the road, having arrived early at the pickup point. I walked out to an outlook on the large section of marsh to the east. Some high ground populated with the marsh shrub community blocked any view of the ocean. The first mosquitoes of the day made their presence known at the edge of the marsh. I walked a little to the south on the road and noticed a lack of disturbance by the fresh pine straw and broken branches covering the path, and wondered about the possibility of this road ending ahead with a path continuing to the south end.

I made my way back to the dike and started the walk across the island. A hunter walked in my direction, and we chatted about our mornings. He and his partner got ten birds and left two in the field that they could not find. We walked on and came upon the next group of hunters before the truck picked us up. In the back of the truck was the hunters' gear and ducks, including gadwalls, shovelers, and a female pintail. Arriving at the dock, the hunters embarked on the three boats for the return to the mainland. I waited for the last boat, riding along and talking with Bill. I learned he had worked on building the new water control structures on Bull Island over the summer. As we headed into the South Santee River on the way back to the landing, I soaked up the environment in my first day on these waters.

The canoe skimmed across the impoundment bearing its cargo of cypress saplings. TNC was implementing a project of replanting cypress trees in the Washo Reserve. The method seemed unusual: to plant the saplings in the open trunks of dead cypress. As a volunteer I did not question the methodology but just pitched in to help. I had walked the Washo's boardwalk and roads before, and leaped at the opportunity to paddle through the Washo and to observe its acclaimed bird life. The clarity of the January day in 2013 and the freedom of our paddled craft set the stage for viewing the Washo. Forty years earlier, another paddler, the writer Peter Matthiessen, shared his perspective on the Washo and the Santee Gun Club.

The deeding of the lands of the Santee Gun Club to TNC in 1974 provoked ambivalence in Matthiessen, a mix of relief and loss. Sale and development of those 24,000 acres had been a possible scenario. Peter Matthiessen, a writer and naturalist, had spent time at the gun club as a guest of his father, the architect and conservationist Evard Matthiessen, and gun club member. The loss? On this last trip to the new South Carolina property in 1974 the son reflected, "What remained across the decade since I had been to the Santee was a rich humus of another time, of a past age in my own life, the silences, the sweet-voiced Gullah blacks in the dark live-oak groves, the resin smell and light of sunny pineland, an ancient cypress swamp and wind and birds, and an old boat called the *Happy Days* that carried gunners to an island on the horizon where the South Santee River meets the sea."[7]

Impounded waters of the Washo Reserve.

On this visit, father and son spent a few days revisiting familiar places. Peter Matthiessen first came to the Santee Gun Club in 1953, and returned almost annually until his last visit in November 1963. Having grown politically distant from the gun club membership, uncomfortable with his privileged life, and disenchanted with killing waterfowl, the final straw for Matthiessen came when members celebrated the assassination of JFK. He never returned, and his father let his membership lapse in 1965. During this 1974 visit they paddled around Murphy Island with familiar guides Johnny and William Garrett. In an interview in 2016, William recalled guiding Peter on Murphy near Ocean Pond to enable Matthiessen's desire to find and shoot a goose. Several things he recalled about Matthiessen: he was a strong paddler (suggesting some members let the guides do all the work), he often sketched wildlife, and "you couldn't get him to shoot a duck over," meaning he would not shoot ducks over the limit.[8]

Another day, Johnny Garrett dropped off the Matthiessens to walk around Murphy on their own. In the younger Matthiessen's visits to the gun club, Murphy Island was the place that moved him the most, and he used the setting Ocean Island in his short story "Traveling Man." On their walk around Murphy, Matthiessen observed it as a changed place, and he experienced "a wave of sadness."

The Matthiessens also visited the Washo Reserve, and set out on the waters in a canoe. Paddling on the impoundment, Matthiessen evoked Washo with the lyrical writing that would win him two future National Book Awards.

> *In the hard light of northwest wind moss sways on the gaunt trunks; gigantic osprey nests top the highest trees like weird growths in the bogs of the Devonian.*
>
> *Dead silence. Bright red leaves spin on the glitter of the water; the canoe paddle drips, and silver drops spread on blue mirrored sky, and the swamp waits.*
>
> *. . . Three pileated woodpeckers, bounding through light and shadow, tighten the stillness with clear clamor; ahead, big turtles slide from low dead logs without a splash. Now all is still. Then a breath of songbirds stirs the cypress branches, half-remembered birds with breasts of the same autumnal reds as the dead cypress needles all around — a company of bluebirds, ten or more. How rare this pretty thrush has seemed in recent years, how wonderful to see it in a cypress swamp. In a quiet, quiet way I am delighted, aware that the oppression felt at the journey's outset has finally dropped away.*[9]

It was reassuring to know that nature had the power to ameliorate the mood of this famed naturalist. With a final reflection he recalled that those fifty days he had spent in the outdoors at the Santee Gun Club over a decade's span were some of the best days of his life.

One feature of the natural world contributing to protection of the Santee Delta has been the abundant populations of biting insects. As the story goes, a proposed Spanish colonization expedition led by Lucas Vázquez de Ayllón into the Santee was aborted due to the inhospitable conditions. The initial manager of Santee Coastal Reserve, Tommy Strange, quipped that visitation is "self-limiting" because of the biting insects. Pierre Manigault had experienced mosquitoes in the northern Alaskan tundra but ranked the Delta mosquitoes as worse.[10]

For some, the swarming of deer flies was a worse fate than mosquitoes. I recalled a trip to Santee Coastal Reserve to ride the bike loop on the Cape with my son Eliot. When we arrived at the parking area, a cloud of deer flies was hammering on our rear window, an effect that journalist Tony Bartelme described on his skin as if being hit by hailstones. After some contemplation Eliot and I braved the flies and flew off on our bikes in an attempt to outrun them. Kenny Williams, former manager of Kinloch Plantation, recalled one particularly horrible incident.

> *I made the mistake of going down a road that I didn't know. Wasn't sure I should be going in there, but I was curious and wanted to see what was back down that road, and I got on a root or something that punctured my tire. And I had a spare. I had a jack and the four-way wrench. But when I got out of the truck to fix the tire, I literally could not do it. There were literally hundreds of deer flies buzzing around me, all of which were trying to bite me at the same time. So I remember just dropping everything and running for my life, which I went back—went about a mile and a half back to the plantation and got some head protection, and I brought somebody back with me to help me do it. And so we got the tire changed. But it was just something one man couldn't stand to do under the circumstances.*[11]

Another significant impact of TNC and other conservation organizations on the Santee Delta has been the use of conservation easements. Ducks Unlimited (DU) is an organization whose main mission is habitat conservation for waterfowl. DU holds the majority of conservation easements in the Delta; TNC and the Lowcountry Land Trust hold others. These conservation easements are donations; property owners give up the rights to subdivide and develop the property though other rights such as farming, timber harvesting, and hunting are maintained. This agreement protects future heirs from high taxes and enables them to maintain ownership.

Peter Manigault, a Delta property owner and conservationist, became a leader in establishing conservation easements on his properties. In the mid-1980s, he established White Oak Forestry, a collective of properties in the lower Santee Delta covering seventeen thousand acres, as an affiliate of Evening Post Industries. As described by the former president of White Oak Forestry, Mike Prevost, "Peter Manigault was a very intelligent, wise, thoughtful individual who was a visionary conservationist, and also a preservationist in the historic preservation area. So his vision was to expand a line of businesses in a manner that would provide diversification of his company's business interest, and at the same time, serve to conserve a very special area of coastal South Carolina, and augment the existing land protection efforts or conservation efforts with White Oak Forestry." Manigault's friend and fellow Delta landowner, Ted Turner, followed suit at Kinloch Plantation with a conservation easement, as did others. One example of the conservation dedication of property owners is Dan Ray, a Georgetown County native. He and his wife bought Annandale Plantation in 2003. The day after the purchase, they placed the entire property under a conservation easement. The protection of a large area through a combination of public lands, and private lands secured by conservation easements, was a model that worked well in the conservation of the ACE Basin, as it has in the Santee Delta.[12]

Overlapping the western corner of the Santee Delta and intimately connected to the ecosystem are the extensive lands of the Francis Marion National Forest, covering around 259,000 acres in total. In 1980 the Forest established four wilderness areas. Wambaw Creek Wilderness connects directly to the Delta, and the creek flows into the South Santee River. At the head of the Wambaw Creek are two other designated wilderness areas, Wambaw Swamp Wilderness and Little Wambaw Swamp Wilderness, both of which are part of the Wambaw watershed. Cypress-gum swamp forest is regenerating in these areas, and the wilderness designation provides protection.

The extensive public lands in the Santee Delta and private lands with conservation easements have created substantial protection for wildlife and habitat. The abundant natural resources of the Delta contributed to a larger section of the coast, from Hobcaw Barony to the north, and south through Cape Romain National Wildlife Refuge and Capers Island, achieving the United Nations Educational, Scientific and Cultural Organization designation as a Biosphere Reserve. UNESCO grants this international recognition to areas both for their natural resources as well as their historic and cultural resources. No Santee Delta site interprets its history more extensively than Hampton Plantation.

Hampton Plantation State Historic Site, part of the South Carolina State Parks system, and acquired from the Rutledge family in 1971, has many claims to fame. It received the designation as a National Historic Landmark initially in

1970. The rigorous process for receiving this designation is only granted for sites that hold national significance. Alternatively, the National Register of Historic Places lists sites that hold state and local significance. Hampton's long and well documented history covers the French Huguenots' emigration and settling along the Santee River; the three Lowcountry families owning Hampton: Horry, Pinckney, and Rutledge; the transformation over the years of a simple house built around 1740 into a plantation mansion; a plantation achieving wealth for its owners through rice cultivation; and the story of the enslaved African Americans providing the labor force for the plantation. One resident, Archibald Rutledge, achieved acclaim through his writing career. His many works often utilized the Santee Delta as a subject, and the state of South Carolina recognized Rutledge as its first poet laureate.

When Rutledge returned to South Carolina after his teaching career in Pennsylvania, he embarked on a large restoration project of the Hampton plantation house alongside the skilled African American artisans living at Hampton. He chronicled this process in his book *Home by the River*. The Horrys built the house between 1730 and 1750, and the structure experienced a number of changes prior to Rutledge's restoration work, beginning in earnest in 1931. The two-and-a-half-story building is of Georgian design, though in 1791 a large, two-story Neoclassical portico was added. The building is of timber frame construction, and part of that frame on the interior is exposed. After transfer to the South Carolina State Parks system, the house has undergone further restoration. Docents currently conduct regular house tours.

Another important building in the vicinity is Brick Church (Wambaw Church), the parish church of St. James Santee. The renovation of this structure has been more recent. In 1972 it too received a National Historic Landmark designation. Church leadership had initiated ongoing work to maintain and repair the building, but water damage, age, and the destructive acts of vandals dictated more substantial efforts. In 1990 vandals wrecked the original black cypress pews in a senseless act. In 1992 a small group formed the St. James Brick Church Restoration Committee, accelerating fundraising and restoration efforts. Brickwork, a new brick and wood fence, a copper roof, and window repairs have been some of the improvements. Two additional projects further protected the church. In 1995 Wambaw Cottage, built next to the church, established a residence for a caretaker. In 2006 TNC acquired a one-hundred-acre parcel of forest, named Wambaw Tract, across the road from the church as a buffer from potential future private development. The Restoration Committee received the transfer of this property, and TNC has held the easement.[13]

East portico column, Brick Church (Wambaw Church).

Besides Hampton Plantation, a number of other plantation homes along the Delta have undergone renovations over the years. Across the rivers from Hampton, the house at Hopsewee Plantation is another National Historic Landmark, built circa 1740. After his parents' purchase of Hopsewee, Phil Wilkinson recalled during his youth an extensive renovation, and the boatbuilding experience of the workers contributed to their quality work. East of Hampton Plantation on the South Santee River, another restored home exists at Harrietta Plantation. Harriott Pinckney Horry, the matriarch at Hampton Plantation, initiated the building of this home as a wedding present for her daughter, Harriott Pinckney Horry Rutledge, upon her marriage to Frederick Rutledge. Other private restored antebellum homes survive along the Santee Delta including Millbrook and the Wedge. Though not a plantation home, but a hunt clubhouse, the Santee Gun Club at Santee Coastal Reserve has also undergone an extensive renovation, and now contains SCDNR offices.[14]

Besides plantation homes, the Santee Delta has a number of other types of restored buildings on public and private lands. The nineteenth century Kitchen House adjacent to the mansion at Hampton Plantation has received both restoration and archaeological study. Restored structures associated with rice culture survive, including a rice threshing barn at Kinloch Plantation, and a brick rice chimney on the North Santee River at Cat Island. The property owners of another existing storm tower out on the Delta have converted it into a hunt clubhouse.

No restoration has occurred on the aforementioned storm tower sitting on public lands. Other brick chimneys from slave dwelling houses still stand in the Delta. The ruins of another notable house, Eldorado, have more protection at Santee Coastal Reserve. Around the same time as the beginning of construction of Harrietta, Rebecca Motte and her son-in-law, Thomas Pinckney, began the building of Eldorado. The house burned in 1897, but the brick ruins remain.[15]

The plantation house at Hampton, as well as the gardens and grounds, have been long-term attractions at this state park. A notable effort at preserving an important part of the African American history at Hampton has been the conserving and supporting of a brick chimney, the only remains of the home lived in by Prince and Sue Alston. The historical interpretation at Hampton has evolved to recount the history of the enslaved population and their descendants. The information for this interpretation has come from archival research, interviews with the descendant African American communities, and ongoing archaeological investigations. One of those archaeological sites studied what turned out to be a slave dwelling dating back to the early nineteenth century. This multiyear investigation unearthed a wealth of information, and an installed three-dimensional viewer enables visitors to "see" the former house. In 2013, community members, students, volunteers, and visitors to the park participated in the Hampton Community Archaeology Project. Interpretive signage around Hampton's grounds has helped visitors understand slavery and rice cultivation, incidents of enslaved individuals escaping to freedom, and the role of enslaved women at Hampton.

When I asked David Jones, archaeologist for the South Carolina State Parks system, the extent of the unearthed remains at Hampton, and specifically how much work remains, he estimated that the work would occupy his successor and several more generations into the future. One search at Hampton has been to locate King Jeremy's Plantation, the historic Sewee Indian settlement on the South Santee River. At this time, the belief is that the remains of this village are not on Hampton's lands but perhaps on an adjacent property. The archaeological investigations at Hampton have been more intensive than anywhere else in the Santee Delta, and thus represent the tip of the iceberg in terms of the unearthed historical record.

The Santee Delta contains several African American communities including Germantown, North Santee, and South Santee, which are inhabited by residents descended from enslaved people. A number of individuals from these communities have worked in the Santee Delta at federal, state, and private operations. Several of the interviewees from the *Voices of the Santee Delta* oral history project were residents of these communities: Henrietta Smalls in Germantown; Gerald Alston, born in Germantown and residing in South Santee; Jane Wineglass in South Santee; and William Garrett, born and raised on Blake's Plantation at the Santee Gun Club, and residing in South Santee. Smalls worked for a time at Hampton. Alston has worked for over three decades at Rochelle Plantation for the Manigaults. Wineglass worked for the Dominicks at the Wedge Plantation. Garrett and two of his brothers were guides at the Santee Gun Club and then at Santee Coastal Reserve. These communities have places of worship (AME and Baptist), and South Santee's Senior Citizen Center provides services and social support for senior community members. These descendant places exist in the wider Gullah Geechee Cultural Heritage Corridor, a Natural Heritage Area, which stretches in the coastal zone from Pender County, North Carolina to St. John's County, Florida.

The *Voices of the Santee Delta* uncovered several examples of mentoring of young white males by senior African American men. Phil Wilkinson discussed his learning from Daddy Ben, a black elder living at Hopsewee during his youth. Daddy Ben taught Wilkinson how to hunt and fish, and gave him his first hound, Diamond. The memories of this mentor inspired Wilkinson to write a poem about him years after his passing. The last line of the poem acknowledges his debt, "I wonder why it's taken so long to know that Daddy Ben is still some part of who I am." Pat Ferris on Cat Island learned to duck hunt from a man he called "Indian"—he identified his ethnicity as African American and Indian. Ferris recalled Indian's ability to call ducks using just his mouth. These two relationships were instances of close and harmonious relationships between white and African American families in the Santee Delta.[16]

Despite the protections already in place, ongoing threats to the Santee Delta exist. While conservation easements have decreased the opportunities for more intensive development, there is not 100 percent coverage in the Delta. At this writing one historic Delta plantation, the Wedge, is for sale, and has no conservation easement. Developers could target the African American communities of the Santee Delta. One specific threat has been the proposal for high voltage power lines to run across the Santee Delta in order to provide higher reliability and increased carrying capacity to the McClellanville area. The federal Rural Utilities Service has studied this project for years and to date has hosted two public hearings (well attended, and with strong opposition to the proposal). While two other routes for these transmission lines are also on the table, a decision has not yet been reached.

An ongoing threat remains for cultural resources in the Delta. The degradation of the Murphy Island storm tower is a sad story. Souvenir seekers endanger this structure, and other remains in the Delta. The lack of protection leaves these sites vulnerable to continuing desecration.

Climate change will be an ongoing threat to the South Carolina coast including the Santee Delta. Saltwater intrusion will continue to progress further into the estuary and change habitat as sea level rises. Changes in salinity have historically occurred through the diversion and rediversion of the Santee as a result of the Santee-Cooper project. This massive hydrologic alteration has also significantly diminished the sediment flow to the coast, and Cedar and Murphy Islands beaches have shrunk as a result. These barrier islands and those of Cape Romain will continue to erode in the face of both sediment loss and sea level rise.

The story of the Santee Delta is one of transformation and resiliency. The natural environment has encountered significant changes periodically. Planters and their enslaved laborers razed the swamp forests to create the fields and infrastructure necessary for rice cultivation. A less radical transition occurred through changing the old rice fields into impoundments conducive for the attraction of migratory waterfowl. Powerful forces impacting the nation in the 1930s led to major hydroelectric projects upstream on the Santee changing the river's hydrology and salinity, not once but twice. Despite the environmental reverberations sustained, the Santee Delta has remained a bountiful natural world through the stewardship on national, state, and private properties.

The account of the resiliency of the peoples of the Santee Delta matches that of the natural world. Many West Africans arriving in the Delta had endured enslavement in their native lands, and the appalling Middle Passage. Those survivors and their descendants experienced the brutal and often fatal conditions of the rice swamps, and the ongoing inhumanity of slavery on their lives. Despite these historic oppressive conditions, the African Americans of the Santee Delta have displayed an indomitable spirit. The people of the descendant communities have demonstrated independence and self-sufficiency in their lives. Many grew up in modern times in the Delta with few conveniences, often living without electricity, running water, or cars. They have exploited the Delta's environment, utilizing its plentiful forest and marine resources. Their faith-based communities have provided its residents with gratitude and optimism in their outlook. The longevity of Sue Alston (110 years) is certainly unrivalled, but many other African Americans of the Delta have lived long lives. One of the interviewees of the *Voices of the Santee Delta*, Henrietta Smalls, had four sisters who like herself all lived into the nineties, and one sister has now lived more than 103 years.

Many private property owners of the Delta plantations have chosen to utilize their resources in stewardship of their lands for a greater good with conservation easements rather than seeking material gain through intensive development. The protection of the environment and cultural resources are vital aspects of the federal and state public lands and their associated facilities. The descendant communities are deeply connected to the lands, waters, and their cultural heritage. The people of the Santee Delta, black and white, have persevered through wars, hurricanes, economic decline, and the residual issues of racial inequity.

Epilogue

The fields of green stretched out a couple miles to the distant tree line— agricultural production on a large scale. It was not the golden acres of rice in the nineteenth century Santee Delta, but modern peanut farming in twenty-first century Calhoun County. These acres were among the over ten thousand peanut acres planted in this county in 2020. Unlike the Delta, these lands displayed a slope toward the north, and the road passing through, Highway 601, descended into the river valley until leveling off on the bridge across the Congaree River. Less than two miles downstream, the Congaree joins with the Wateree from the north to form the Santee River. To the west of the bridge lies the majority of the twenty thousand acres of the Congaree National Park.

I traveled to these public lands on another ninety-degree August day. Like others, I came to this National Park, the self-described "Home of Champions," for its acclaimed big trees, including some national and state champions. My specific goal was to view a small section of swamp forest, composed of mature cypress and tupelo gum trees. Finding this swamp forest remnant was challenging, since flooding and tree fall damage had closed a number of trails. But guided by a map with notes on closures, local knowledge, and the experience of a past visit, I set out on the low boardwalk.

I had the trail to myself, and soaked in the dappled light suffusing the midmorning forest. The trees' canopy buffered the sun's heat, and the place had a quiet serenity. I did not have to venture far to encounter some of the giant trees of the bottomland hardwood forest. Specimens of loblolly pine and sweetgum towered overhead, and though these species are common on my Awendaw property, the Congaree trees dwarfed mine.

I did not see another person until the boardwalk turned into a ground path. A drought had finally dried up the floodplain forest floor allowing walking on these trails. A voice sounded in the distance, and it resolved into the call of a barred owl. A tent stood on a site overlooking Wise Lake, and I continued on the Oakridge Trail to the end of the lake. I had walked this Oakridge loop back in 2018, and recalled this section below the trail being flooded. But on this day the forest floor was dry, and I stepped off the beaten path to walk amongst the trees.

This parcel of swamp forest was not large, and comparable to the area of my own property's three and a half acres. Yet these trees were giants. The buttressed bases of the tupelos were massive, and cypress knees populated sections of the muddy ground. The floor was open between trees excluding the cypress knees, and the wide spacing of trees was a function of the distribution algorithm. This forest community gave a miniature approximation of that prehistoric Santee

Swamp forest in Congaree National Park.

Delta ecosystem, but it was a major leap of imagination to picture the original ten thousand acres of this forest occupying the Delta.

The Wateree that borders the far eastern end of Congaree National Park is the other main trunk that sources the Santee River. The extensive eastern network of the Santee has a number of headwaters. The head with the highest elevation in this Carolina river system are those waters that run off Grandfather Mountain's southern faces. The corresponding waters on the far side of the mountain's ridge, marking the Eastern Continental Divide, flow in an opposite direction toward the Mississippi River and Gulf of Mexico.

With great disappointment, I scuttled plans for a spring 2020 mountain trip and a plan to walk up to Grandfather Mountain's apex, Calloway Peak, located on the Eastern Continental Divide. Somewhere on those slopes are the beginnings of the Linville River, which downstream connects into the Catawba/Wateree system. Hiking the trail up to the summit would have to wait for a future date.

In considering these planned explorations, I recalled visits to the vicinity almost fifty years ago. When discovering the Appalachian Mountains in my college days, the place that had the most attraction and impact was Linville Gorge. I experienced the rich ecosystems, a National Wilderness Area, the adventures possible with backpacking, and the gorge, a pocket canyon known as the "Grand Canyon of the East." I knew the geology was impressive by the mountains on each side of the gorge, and a towering rock formation in the middle—the Chimneys, a pinnacle climbable without technical equipment. I did not know the Cherokee name for the Linville, "Eeseeoh," meaning river of many cliffs. Linville Gorge was a discovery of my young adult years, and it was not until the last decade that I came to understand that those waters of the Linville, cutting through that canyon, flowed toward the Santee Delta.

The closing of businesses resulting from the pandemic included the Audubon Center at Beidler Forest in Harleyville, South Carolina. The 1,763-acre virgin swamp forest is part of Four Holes Swamp. These waters do not connect to the Santee system, but are part of the Edisto River watershed. My previous self-study of the swamp forest community was a review of the 1981 published survey of the Beidler Forest by Citadel botany professor Richard Porcher. When I learned of the limited re-opening (reduced numbers of visitors and days open) of the boardwalk through the forest, I made plans to visit Beidler.

The short trail into Beidler's 1.75-mile boardwalk began on upland by the closed visitor center, and then transitioned into bottomland hardwood forest. The prevalence of dwarf palmetto indicated the higher elevation compared to what I would find ahead. I soon entered the flooded swamp forest, and the stands of mature cypress and tupelo. Flooded is a relative term in the swamp, since the seasonal variation is great. Markers along the boardwalk noted the flood level of the great inundation in 2015. Signage also documented the destruction to the forest caused by Hurricane Hugo here in 1989, and the variable level of canopy loss: 80 percent of upland, 10 percent of cypress sites.

This swamp was the forest community once populating the Santee Delta. The Beidler Forest has a more specific ecosystem name: a blackwater cypress-tupelo creek swamp, differing from the Santee Delta swamp forest that was predominantly brownwater with tidal influence. Yet the species and forest were similar, and gave a good feel for the distribution of trees. The smaller acreage of swamp forest in my visit to Congaree was dwarfed by the more than seventeen hundred acres here.

The canopy heights varied with the tree diversity distributed throughout the forest. Creeks would have provided the easiest passage for indigenous people and early explorers through this challenging wilderness. The visual density of the forest contrasted with the acoustics. The quiet was profound, and only brief-

Swamp forest in Audubon's Beidler Forest Sanctuary.

ly disturbed by the scream of a preadolescent visitor. At one stop, the patter of falling leaves was a soft gentle rustling of the sonic world.

Individuals of the Beidler Forest shined. There was no appearance from the "mascot" of Beidler. National parks and refuges regularly market their identity from a flagship or charismatic species: Great Smoky Mountains National Park has the black bear, Waccamaw National Wildlife Refuge has the swallow-tailed kite, and Beidler has the prothonotary warbler, a beautiful golden flash in the swamp. Many old growth cypress and tupelo invited a closer look. A labeled tree was unfamiliar to me - pumpkin ash *Fraxinus profunda* – and I checked later with staff to make sure it was not a Halloween spoof. Besides the magnificent individual trees, a duo caught my eye. Two trees were joined "at the hip," and I viewed and photographed from various angles this cypress and sweetgum union. I have marveled at various conjoined trees in nature.

Though not a mascot, the water moccasin is a charismatic species (for some) at Beidler, and the reception staff person had alerted me to an individual hanging out around marker #18 on the boardwalk. I had forgotten to be on the alert, but saw the movement as the sizable reptile dropped off the planking into the water. Its submerged body was visible on the bottom, its distinctive markings showing through the tannin-stained waters. I waited to point out the snake to two other visitors coming along before completing the loop walk.

I made a Saturday visit to an island on Labor Day weekend. But this island was no tourist destination, unless you were in a car speeding to an island beach to the north or south, past the Santee Delta – Pawley's Island? Myrtle Beach? Isle of Palms? I pulled off the causeway raising the Ocean Highway (US 17) above the wetlands of the Santee Delta between the North and South Santee Rivers, and drove down into the parking lot of the Santee Delta Wildlife Management Area (WMA) East. The relatively steep slope to the parking was not a natural terrain feature, and it was no surprise that I found no other cars.

So what island was this, sitting between the rivers? No signs posted its name, Lynch's Island. Jonah Lynch emigrated from Ireland in 1677, and his son Thomas (1675 – 1752) received grants for a number of properties on the North and South Santee Rivers, to become valuable plantations including Hopsewee, Fairfield, and Peachtree. He also acquired a fourteen-hundred-acre island between the north and south rivers, bordered on the east by Sixmile Creek, and to the west by Push and Go Creek. It became known as Lynches Island, and is another of those hidden features of the Delta.[1]

A manmade elevation of the Santee Delta interrupting the horizontal nature of the land is the Highway 17 causeway. The Lynch family, including three generations of Thomas Lynch, had a prominent role in changing the island landscape. The ferries established for the crossing of the North and Santee Rivers had utilized Push and Go Creek for the passage, but a board of commissioners had authorized a building of a causeway to traverse Lynches Island. Thomas Lynch contracted with the Commons House of Assembly to carry out this work, and Lynch's Causeway was completed in 1741. This roadway had problems, and the third generation Thomas Lynch (1749–1779) worked on a new causeway in the 1770s. In 1774, Hugh Finlay, surveying the roads, was crossing the old causeway when his horse "sunk between the logs up to the belly." One traveler observed in his crossing in 1778 that many enslaved laborers were working, and that the old and new causeways were barely passable. A later survey of the causeway in 1825 noted that flooding events overtopped the roadbed, and after draining left a slippery mess. [2]

The modern causeway elevating Highway 17 over the Delta has functioned as a two-mile-long dam for the Santee waters. There is a large salinity difference between the waters above and below the causeway, with the waters above mainly fresh. During some major floods in South Carolina, the causeway has held back a large portion of floodwaters released from the Santee dam from the lower Delta.[3]

At the Santee Delta WMA East parking lot, two signs provided some limited information on visits beyond the locked gate to the unpaved roadway: no motorized vehicles were allowed, and foot traffic was welcome except during the migratory waterfowl season, November 1 to February 8. In 2011, I walked around the whole perimeter of this WMA on an early April day when the roadways were not overgrown. Today would be no walk in the park.

There was no evidence of previous foot traffic as I started out, and the uncut growth was ankle height and above. Soon the deer flies and mosquitoes found me. I had dressed to cover up as much skin as possible, though my hands were particularly vulnerable to the bites of deer flies. I pulled up a pandemic-purchased neck gaiter over my ears and face, but found the flies were able to bite through the cloth. The dike I walked paralleling the North Santee River had a border of small and large cypress trees. I kept on until the first dike heading across the open wetlands of the Delta, and hoped to find some relief from the biting insects in that direction.

The deer flies stayed with me as I left the forested border along the river, and would continue with me for the remainder of the walk. Though bothersome, the discomfort was not such where, at the worst, I would need to turn around and run. Besides clothing, I utilized two other related strategies for coping with the biting insects: acclimatization, and an old cognitive strategy shared with me by Phil Wilkinson, "Well, if you don't pay them no mind, they won't worry you." As I ventured out on the dike through wetlands that once were rice fields, the vista opened up all the way across to the South Santee River and the uplands beyond. The house on the bluff at Fairfield was visible.

The SCDNR map showed about forty impoundments in the Santee Delta WMA East, each representing a former rice field. Early September was a time of rice harvest. Heat, high humidity, and biting insects would have been part of that work environment. Overseers would have exerted immense pressure to harvest the carefully tended rice crop and move it to a safe location out of the weather.

A single cypress tree appeared as a sentinel in the open wetlands. The Delta once would have contained around ten thousand acres of swamp forest of cypress and tupelo gum, with the cypress canopy looming overhead at over one hundred feet, and the gums not far behind in height. What a different world – a forested wetland and a shadowy forest floor. My visits to Congaree and Beidler gave an idea of that primeval forest.

Lines of shrubs and trees marking other banks interrupted the wetlands panorama, and my loop path back to the Highway 17 causeway and parking lot

A lone cypress and canal out in the Santee Delta WMA.

appeared ahead. Before arriving at that final dike, I became aware of a missing object, a map contained in a plastic bag. With no desire to backtrack, but with a commitment to leave no trace, I made the return walk, finally recovering the dropped item near the lone cypress. Although my parked vehicle was near, I opted to complete the longer loop walk.

When I finally arrived at the dike to turn toward the causeway, I realized this bank paralleled Garfish Creek, and followed the natural creek curves. The frustration of the long backtrack was gone, and along this bank I stumbled upon a reward: the golden sighting of first one, and then a pair of prothonotary warblers *Protonotaria citrea*. The Latin *citrea* is lemon, the ripe fruit of which captures this warbler's color. The earlier challenging conditions and discomfort on Lynches Island dissipated.

I began my walk at the entrance to the Santee Coastal Reserve, and headed away from the reserve and out to the South Santee Road. On the curve past the South Santee Senior and Community Center and Lily Pond Missionary Baptist Church, the road crossed Collins Creek. Leaves floated by as water flowed under the bridge, and a distinctive cypress towered above the road on the left. Indigenous names for the creek included Washaw and Washasha. My path followed in the paths of several past community members on their way to work.

The Collins Creek community is a smaller section of the greater South Santee area. It was the birthplace of Jane Wineglass, and a home during her life. Jane was the fifteenth and youngest child of Sambo Green and Eve Manigault Green. Jane's mother was born on Murphy Island, and worked for years as a cook at the Wedge Plantation. According to Jane, she was "everybody's momma," and was known in the community as Momma Eve or Auntie Eve. Walking with Jane to the Wedge, her mother would be constantly praying for the sick. She walked to work until disability ended her employment, and Jane followed in her footsteps as a cook at the Wedge. During Jane's childhood she visited the Wedge often, since several of her adult siblings and their families resided and worked there.[4]

Jane's mother cooked for the Wedge's manager, prior to Richard Dominick, a retired New York ophthalmologist, purchasing the property in 1966. He and his wife Tatiana moved in to a former slave dwelling, "the Wedgling," while the main house was renovated. Dominick developed a love for the Lowcountry in his childhood when he visited his parents' plantation in Coosawhatchie, South Carolina. Dominick had a lifelong passion for studying and collecting moths. He recognized the diversity of moths in the Santee Delta, and his collection included the southernmost range of the northern moth species, and the northernmost range of the southern species. Dominick was an amateur entomologist, and hosted many visitors to the Wedge, including scientists and amateur moth collectors. He built a laboratory, nicknamed the Bug House, to collect and photograph moths. Dominick also set up the Wedge Entomological Research Foundation, with such notable patrons as Prince Phillip, Roger Tory Peterson, Sir Peter Scott, and David Rockefeller.[5]

Jane Wineglass was effusive in her praise of Dominick, describing him as a prize. She recalled how each summer he would put on an event for the people of South Santee. The Dominicks took Jane on a six-week trip to London where they had a home, and that "glorious" experience was a highlight of her life. Dominick's stepdaughter Stephanie Waldron recalled Jane as a wonderful person, "She's one of the most beautiful people you'll ever see." In talking to Jane in 2015, I was also impressed with her spirit, energy, humor, and faith.

The Wedge was one of the prominent rice plantations of the Santee Delta, and the home plantation of William Lucas, the son of Jonathan Lucas, the noted millwright and inventor of the first rice pounding mill. Completed in 1826, the two-story house over a brick basement with twenty rooms and distinctive finish inside and out was a symbol of the wealth Lucas earned through rice planting. The name for the plantation derives from the pie-shaped property with the wide side on the South Santee River. The property also included valuable lands, Blackwood, out on the Santee Delta and located on another island, Atkinson's.

The Lucas family sold the Wedge in 1929, and there were two intervening owners prior to Dominick's purchase. After Richard Dominick's passing in 1976, his wife sold the Wedge to University of South Carolina in 1982, and the facility became the International Center for Public Health Research. A main focus of study and training for professionals from developing countries was the control of vector borne diseases particularly carried by mosquitoes. Mosquitoes thrived at the Wedge, since the building of impoundments throughout the Santee Delta increased the habitat conducive for mosquito larvae. Federal funding for the program ran out, and the center closed in the mid-1990s. Previous efforts by USC to sell the Wedge were not successful, with a 2014 sale price of four million dollars finding no buyers. *The Post and Courier* documented the decline of the 1826 house, described as "demolition by neglect," and an editorial on January 23, 2020, pushed USC to either use the Wedge or sell it. One half to a million dollars was the estimated renovation cost of the Lucas house. Later in August USC put the Wedge again on the market for sale, accepting sealed bids. A buyer committed to conservation and preservation of the house was an ultimate goal. The sale was made in late 2020, and it appears the new owner intends to renovate the home and care for the lands.

Another large property in the Santee Delta was also listed for sale in August. Big Commander Island, in the upper Santee Delta, between the North and South Santee River, was advertised as 1964 acres of "unencumbered and undeveloped Santee Delta river front." This Delta tract presented less possible development opportunity than the Wedge due to its island status without access by a bridge. In 2021, the Open Space Institute and The Nature Conservancy jointly acquired Commander Island. SCDNR will manage the property after its transfer.

As Jane had mentioned, it was a fifteen-minute walk to the Wedge, the entrance next to Harrietta Plantation. The sharp end of the Wedge leaves little of the property on the South Santee Road, and property markers for Fairfield Plantation were posted all along the road on both sides up to Highway 17. I was fortunate on this day not to be bothered by biting insects, and without need to resort to Jane Wineglass's method of coping – breaking a branch off a bush and swatting them. Across from the large brick gates at the entrance to Harrietta is the South Santee Cemetery. Walking on the left along the graveyard, I was surprised when I saw the tombstone "Jane Green Wineglass." I had wondered if she might be interred here, and had planned to stop on my return to search. My path was now following the steps of Sambo Green, Jane's father, when he made a daily one-way four-mile walk to Hampton Plantation when building a rice trunk for Archibald Rutledge.

The road crossed the busy Highway 17, and the name changed to Rutledge Road. I have driven this road, South Santee and Rutledge, many times, but on foot some subtle features became apparent. The roadway undulated with topography, alluvial ridges and valleys exposed by walking, and reflected in different forest communities. Young longleaf pines grew along the road marking the recovery after an uncontrolled wildfire devastated the White Oak Forestry lands a decade ago. A section of live oaks bordering a gated forest roadway indicated a former plantation entrance, Peachtree.

I would have missed the wildflowers along the roadway if traveling by car, and the variety grew the more I observed. Goldenrod, narrowleaf sunflowers, and spectacular yellow fringed orchids sprinkled the roadside with shades of yellow. The first fall foliage change, the scarlet of young black gums, appeared along the forest edge, and coral bean added color. The limited traffic, mostly coming from Germantown, allowed for a quiet walk. A gradual slope descended to Montgomery Creek, another small stream draining swamplands and emptying into the South Santee River a little over a mile to the east. The slight climb after the creek led to a prominent crossing.

Rutledge Road intersected the Georgetown Road, formerly known before the Revolution as the Old King's Highway. To the left and two miles down this sandy road lies Brick Church. To the right and past the gate through White Oak Forestry property and a mile to the bank of the South Santee River exists the location of Isaac Mazyck's eighteenth-century ferry landing. Those properties near this intersection, and between Rutledge Road and the river, were the former Montgomery and Romney Plantations.

Hampton Plantation was not far ahead. The entrance was sandy and gradually descended into the Santee River valley. Arriving at the empty parking lot, I encountered just one staff member, mowing acres of grass. In a walkaround, I passed the Big House on a river bluff, and the Kitchen House. From there the grounds sloped to the edge of Hampton Creek. I imagined Francis Marion's nighttime swim across to Hampton Island to escape Tarleton. I continued to the Kitchen Field rice trunk and dike replaced in 2018 with modern equipment, including a trackhoe and dump truck doing the heavy lifting. That project was a marked contrast to Sambo Green's trunk construction and installation occurring around seventy-five years ago.

Coming around toward the parking lot, I stopped at the conserved and supported chimney of the house of Prince and Sue Alston. This central chimney with back-to-back fire boxes and hearths was a reminder of other extant double-hearth chimneys out in the Santee Delta. A sign displayed photos of the house, Sue Alston and her son Will; content recounted their legacy to Hampton Plantation. Bluebirds perched on a wire near the mowed corridor between meadows leading down to the slave dwelling house site, and an old rice field past it, Mainfield.

Throughout the Santee Delta and beyond in the Lowcountry, individual rice fields have their own identities and names. Enslaved people and their descendants have expressed ownership of these sites of toil. Charles Joyner described this paradox, and recounted examples in the Waccamaw Neck area. The ex-slave Morris informed the new landowner of Hobcaw Barony, financier Bernard Baruch, "De strength of dese arms and dese legs and of dis old back, Mist' Bernie, is in your rice banks. ... No, Mist' Bernie, you ain't agoin' to run old Morris off dis place." And J. Motte Alston asserted that his lead man, Cudjo, "looked upon my property as belonging to him." It seems that Prince, Sue, and Will Alston all shared an attitude of ownership at Hampton beyond their employment.[6]

On a side road off the exit road, an African American cemetery lies on what is known as Sam Hill, an inholding in the state park. The descendant community of Germantown still uses the cemetery for burials, and I noted a new stone marking the grave of a Germantown resident who passed away earlier in the year. Sue Alston was also interred there. She had stated in a 1976 interview that she would be lying down in the future at Hampton, and her spirit would continue there.

The return walk gave further opportunity for introspection, a benefit of foot travel. What would Sambo Green's thoughts have been on his walk home to Collins Creek? Would he have been planning the next steps in his trunk construction? Maybe he had speculated about his evening meal, or wondered about his children? Perhaps when he returned home he would need to spend time in his garden, or would go fishing. Horrys, Pinckneys, and Rutledges riding by wagon or carriage would have traveled this same path to the Georgetown Road on the way to Wambaw Church. George Washington on his 1791 southern tour would have also passed here on his way to Hampton. Other historic figures would have utilized the path, including King Jeremy and the Sewees.

I stopped at the South Santee Cemetery to pay my respects to Jane Wineglass. There were other Greens in the cemetery, several who appeared to be Jane's family members. I had interviewed her in December 2015 at the South Santee Senior and Community Center, and saw on her stone that she passed away in October 2017. There was a short epitaph, "Constant of faith Generous of heart." She was certainly a woman of faith, as was her mother, and I had passed their house of worship back in Collins Creek, Greater Zion AME Church. "Generous of heart" was most accurate, and she was extremely generous to share her story with me. I could still hear in my mind parts of the interview: her laughter, her mimicking her beloved mother. I can always return to her voice, recorded, and accessible to all.

Jane Wineglass, 2015.

NOTES

Prologue

1. Charles Kovacik and John Winberry, *South Carolina: A Geography* (Boulder: Westview Press, 1987), 27.

2. Though Delta often refers to the Mississippi Delta, this narrative will often use "Delta" for Santee Delta.

3. Chester DePratter and Val Green, "John Lawson and the Great Catawba Trading Path," *Carologue* 16, no. 3 (autumn 2000), 16.

4. John Lawson, *A New Voyage to Carolina* (London, 1709), 25, 27.

5. Patricia Nichols, *Voices of Our Ancestors* (Columbia: University of South Carolina Press, 2009), 54, 68; Lorenzo D. Turner, *Africanisms in the Gullah Dialect* (Chicago: University of Chicago Press, 1949. Reprint, Columbia: University of South Carolina Press, 2001), 2.

6. The spelling "Charleston" will be used throughout the narrative, except when quoted.

The Prehistoric Delta

1. Wharton et al., "The Ecology of Bottomland Hardwood Swamps of the Southeast: A Community Profile," U.S. Fish and Wildlife Service, Biological Services Program, Washington, DC FWS/OBS-81/37, 31, https://ecos.fws.gov/ServCat/DownloadFile/105358?Reference=65824.

2. Wilbur Mattoon, *The Southern Cypress*, Bulletin no. 272 (Washington, DC: U.S. Department of Agriculture, 1915), 2.

3. William Bartram, *The Travels of William Bartram: Naturalist's Edition,* rev. ed. (Athens: University of Georgia Press, 1998), 90–91.

4. John Lawson, *A New Voyage to Carolina* (London, 1709), 117–18; John Dennis, *The Great Cypress Swamps* (Baton Rouge: Louisiana State University Press, 1988), 1.

5. Richard D. Porcher, "The Vascular Flora of the Francis Beidler Forest in Four Holes Swamp, Berkeley and Dorchester Counties, South Carolina," *Castanea* 46, no. 4 (1981): 261, www.jstor.org/stable/4032963.

6. Porcher, "Vascular Flora," 264.

7. Lawson, *A New Voyage to Carolina*, 27–29.

8. Miles Hayes and Jacqueline Michel, *A Coast for All Seasons: A Naturalist's Guide to the Coast of South Carolina* (Columbia: Pandion Books, 2008), 155, 160–62.

9. Kevin G. Stewart and Mary-Russell Roberson, *Exploring the Geology of the Carolinas: A Field Guide to Favorite Places from Chimney Rock to Charleston* (Chapel Hill: University of North Carolina Press, 2017), 33–42.

10. Björn Kjerfve and Jeffrey E. Greer, "Hydrography of the Santee River During Moderate Discharge Conditions," *Estuaries* 1, no. 2 (June 1978): 111, https://doi.org/10.2307/1351600.

11. Lawson, *A New Voyage to Carolina*, 22.

12. Bartram, *The Travels of William Bartram*, 147; Mark Kinzer, *Nature's Return: An Environmental History of Congaree National Park* (Columbia: University of South Carolina Press, 2017), 24–25.

13. Steven G. Platt, Christopher G. Brantley, and Thomas R. Rainwater, "Native American Ethnobotany of Cane (Arundinaria spp.) in the Southeastern United States: A Review," *Castanea* 74, no. 3 (September 2009): 272–77.

14. I described this historic route through creeks and bays from the Santee to Charleston Harbor in the final chapter of *Tracing the Cape Romain Archipelago*.

15. Christopher T. Espenshade and Paul E. Brockington, Jr., "An Archaeological Study of the Minim Island Site 38GE46, Georgetown County, SC: Early Woodland Dynamics in Coastal SC," Brockington and Associates, 1989 (tDAR id: 391068); https://doi.org/10.6067/XCV80C4WM2.

16. Blair A. Rudes, "Place Names of Cofitachequi," *Anthropological Linguistics* 46, no. 4 (Winter 2004): 359–60, http://www.jstor.org/stable/30029015; Chester DePratter, "Cofitachequi," in *The Forgotten Centuries: Indians and Europeans in the American South, 1521–1704*, ed. Charles Hudson and Carmen Tesser (Athens: University of Georgia Press, 1994), 203–4.

17. Fred C. Rhode, Rudolph G. Arndt, Jeffrey W. Foltz, and Joseph M. Quattro, *Freshwater Fishes of South Carolina* (Columbia: University of South Carolina Press, 2009), 70; Kinzer, *Nature's Return*, 196; Charles Ball, *Slavery in the United States: A Narrative of the Life and Adventures of Charles Ball, a Black Man* (New York: Negro Universities Press, 1969), 292–96.

The Command of Water

1. Andrea Wulf, *The Brother Gardeners: Botany, Empire, and the Birth of an Obsession* (New York: Vintage Books, 2008), 25–26; John Bartram, "Diary of a Journey through the Carolinas, Georgia, and Florida, from July 1, 1765, to April 10, 1766," *Transactions of the American Philosophical Society*, n.s., 33, no. 1, Philadelphia (1942): 22, https://www.jstor.org/stable/1005551.

2. S. Max Edelson, *Plantation Enterprise in Colonial South Carolina* (Cambridge, MA: Harvard University Press, 2006), 103; Richard D. Porcher, Jr. and William R. Judd, *The Market Preparation of Carolina Rice: An Illustrated History of Innovations in the Lowcountry Rice Kingdom* (Columbia: University of South Carolina Press, 2014), 30, 41, 52.

3. Miles Hayes and Jacqueline Michel, *A Coast for all Seasons: A Naturalist's Guide to the Coast of South Carolina* (Columbia: Pandion Books, 2008), 58; Porcher and Judd, *Market Preparation*, 61.

4. Porcher and Judd, *Market Preparation*, 65–67; Judith A. Carney, *Black Rice* (Cambridge, MA: Harvard University Press, 2001), 92–94.

5. William Bartram, *The Travels of William Bartram: Naturalist's Edition*, rev. ed. (Athens: University of Georgia Press, 1998), 58; David Doar, *Rice and Rice Planting in the South Carolina Low Country*, Contributions from the Charleston Museum, no. 8 (Charleston: Charleston Museum, 1936), 8–9; J. Motte Alston, *Rice Planter and Sportsman: The Recollections of J. Motte Alston, 1821–1909*, ed. Arney R. Childs (Columbia: University of South Carolina Press, 1953), 58.

6. Porcher and Judd, *Market Preparation*, 67; Alston, *Rice Planter and Sportsman*, 119.

7. Daniel C. Littlefield, *Rice and Slaves: Ethnicity and the Slave Trade in Colonial South Carolina* (Chicago: University of Illinois Press, 1981), 74–75.

8. Porcher and Judd, *Market Preparation*, 67–68.

9. Jane Wineglass, interview by Bob Raynor, December 14, 2015, *Voices of the Santee Delta* oral history project (hereinafter cited as VSD), 16; Archibald Rutledge, *God's Children* (Charleston: History Press, 2009), 8.

10. Rutledge, 9–10.

11. Doar, *Rice and Rice Planting*, 13–15.

12. William Garrett, interview by Bob Raynor, June 14, 2016, VSD, 2.

13. Phil Wilkinson, interview by Bob Raynor, January 25, 2016, VSD, 45–46; Bill Mace, interview by Bob Raynor, December 6, 2015, VSD, 13; John Bartram, "Diary of a Journey," 22; John Lane and Philip Wilkinson, *Seven Days on the Santee Delta* (Charleston: Evening Post Books, 2020), 42.

14. John Scott Strickland, "'No More Mud Work': The Struggle for the Control of Labor and Production in Low Country South Carolina, 1863–1880," in *The Southern Enigma: Essays on Race, Class, and Folk Culture*, ed. Walter J. Fraser, Jr. and Winfred B. Moore, Jr. (Westport, CT: Greenwood Press, 1983), 48.

15. Rutledge, *God's Children*, 12.

16. Peter H. Wood, *Black Majority* (New York: W. W. Norton, 1974), 56–62; Carney, *Black Rice*, 27, 89.

17. Charles Joyner, *Down by the Riverside: A South Carolina Slave Community* (Urbana: University of Illinois Press, 1984), 43–45; Porcher and Judd, *Market Preparation*, 37–40.

18. Porcher and Judd, *Market Preparation*, 87.

19. Porcher and Judd, *Market Preparation*, 83; Mark M. Newell, "Small Craft of the Low Country Rice Culture," appendix 3, in William C. Fleetwood, Jr., *Tidecraft: The Boats of South Carolina, Georgia, and Northeastern Florida, 1550–1950* (Tybee Island, GA: WBG Marine Press, 1995), 311.

20. George C. Rogers, Jr., *The History of Georgetown County, South Carolina* (Columbia: University of South Carolina Press, 1970), 43–44.

21. Henry Savage, Jr. and Elizabeth J. Savage, *André and François Michaux* (Charlottesville: University Press of Virginia, 1986), 104.

22. Archibald Henderson, *Washington's Southern Tour 1791* (Cambridge, MA: Riverside Press, 1923), 137.

23. Anne B. L. Bridges, and Roy Williams III, *St. James Santee Plantation Parish: History and Records, 1685–1925* (Spartanburg, SC: Reprint Company, 1997), 87–88.

24. Lynn B. Harris, *Patroons & Periaguas: Enslaved Watermen and Watercraft of the Lowcountry* (Columbia: University of South Carolina Press, 2014), 48–49, 57; Philip M. Hamer, George C. Rogers Jr., C. James Taylor, and David R. Chesnutt, eds., and Peggy J. Clark, ed. asst., *The Papers of Henry Laurens* (hereinafter cited as *Laurens Papers*), 15 vols. (Columbia: University of South Carolina Press, 1972–1998), 4: 616.

25. "Thirty Dollars Reward," *City* (Charleston) *Gazette*, November 16, 1795.

26. *Laurens Papers*, vol. 4, HL to John Gray, July 24, 1765, 657.

27. Harris, *Patroons & Periaguas*, 48.

28. John Lawson, *A New Voyage to Carolina* (London, 1709), 18–24.

29. Charles Ball, *Slavery in the United States: A Narrative of the Life and Adventures of Charles Ball, a Black Man* (New York: Negro Universities Press, 1969), 292.

30. Lawson, *A New Voyage,* 22; Fleetwood, *Tidecraft*, 31.

31. R. Nicholas Olsberg, "Ship Registers in the South Carolina Archives; 1734–1780," *South Carolina Historical Magazine* 74 (1973), 189–279 passim.

32. Carney, *Black Rice*, 31.

33. Roy Williams III and Alexander L. Lofton, *Rice to Ruin: The Jonathan Lucas Family in South Carolina 1783–1929* (Columbia: University of South Carolina Press, 2018), 391–92.

34. Hayden R. Smith, *Carolina's Golden Fields: Inland Rice Cultivation in the South Carolina Lowcountry, 1670–1860* (Cambridge, UK: Cambridge University Press, 2020), 84; Suzanne C. Linder, and Marta L. Thacker, *Historical Atlas of the Rice Plantations of Georgetown County and the Santee River* (Columbia: South Carolina Department of Archives and History for the Historic Ricefields Association, 2001), 728, 642; Porcher and Judd, *Market Preparation*, 3.

Wambaw

1. Gene Waddell, *Indians of the South Carolina Lowcountry 1562–1751* (Spartanburg, SC: Reprint Company, 1980), 219; Susan B. Bates and Harriott C. Leland, *French Santee: A Huguenot Settlement in Colonial South Carolina* (Baltimore: Otter Bay Books, 2015), 180, n971.

2. Walter Edgar, *South Carolina: A History* (Columbia: University of South Carolina Press, 1998), 50–51; Bates and Leland, *French Santee*, 7.

3. Bates and Leland, *French Santee*, 168–69.

4. Roy Williams III and Alexander L. Lofton, *Rice to Ruin: The Jonathan Lucas Family in South Carolina, 1783–1929* (Columbia: University of South Carolina Press, 2018), 69, 74–75.

5. Anne B. L. Bridges and Roy Williams III, *St. James Santee Plantation Parish: History and Records, 1685–1925* (Spartanburg, SC: Reprint Company, 1997), 4; Bates and Leland, *French Santee*, 25.

6. Robert Morgan, personal communication with the author, April 2020.

7. Caroline Moore, ed., *Abstracts of the Wills of the State of South Carolina, 1760–1784*, (Columbia: R.L. Bryan, 1969), 3:320.

8. Bridges and Williams, *St. James Santee*, 51 n104, 361.

9. S. Max Edelson, *Plantation Enterprise in Colonial South Carolina* (Cambridge, MA: Harvard University Press, 2006), 203.

10. *The Papers of Henry Laurens* (hereinafter cited as *Laurens Papers*), Philip M. Hamer et al., eds., vol. 1 (Columbia: University of South Carolina Press, 1968), xiv.

11. Edelson, *Plantation Enterprise*, Appendix Table A.13, 284; *Laurens Papers*, George C. Rogers and David R. Chestnutt, eds., vol. 3, Henry Laurens (HL) to John Coming Ball, Jan. 7, 1763, 208; *Laurens Papers*, vol. 5, HL to Abraham Schad, October 1, 1765, 12.

12. *Laurens Papers*, vol. 4, HL to John Knight, August 24, 1764, 378; HL to Cowes & Harford, September 10, 1764, 411; vol. 5, HL to Abraham Schad, February 1, 1766, 62; Edelson, *Plantation Enterprise*, 241.

13. *Laurens Papers*, vol. 4, HL to Paul Douxsaint, July 18, 1765, 655.

14. *City Gazette*, November 26, 1787.

15. *Laurens Papers*, vol. 4, HL to John Coming Ball, November 29, 1763, 59.

16. *Laurens Papers*, vol. 4, HL to Joseph Brown, July 24, 1765, 658.

17. *Laurens Papers*, vol. 6, Appendix B, 611–12.

18. Jeffrey W. Gardner, and Eric C. Poplin, "Historic Adaptations Through Time: Archaeological Testing of Five Sites, Francis Marion National Forest, Berkeley and Charleston Counties, South Carolina," report by Brockington and Associates, 1992, 88. (tDAR id: 156118). Report copy provided by Robert Morgan, Francis Marion National Forest.

19. Gardner and Poplin, 110, 117, 128.

20. Gardner and Poplin, 131–33.

21. Ball, *Slaves in the* Family, 217.

22. Ball, 217.

23. Robert Lambert, *South Carolina Loyalists in the American Revolution* (Columbia: University of South Carolina Press, 1987), 113–15; Bridges and Williams, *St. James Santee*, 75–76; Ball, *Slaves in the* Family, 217.

24. Edgar, *South Carolina: A History*, 238.

25. Samuel Dubose, and Frederick A. Porcher, *A Contribution to the History of the Huguenots of South Carolina, Consisting of Pamphlets*, ed. Theodore G. Thomas (New York: the Knickerbocker Press, 1887), 16–18; Ball, *Slaves in the Family*, 231.

26. John Oller, *The Swamp Fox: How Francis Marion Saved the American Revolution* (Boston, MA: Da Capo Press, 2016), 201.

27. Oller, 213, 220–21; John W. Gordon, *South Carolina and the American Revolution: A Battlefield History* (Columbia: University of South Carolina Press, 2003), 172.

28. Oller, 214–15; Edgar, *South Carolina*, 239.

29. Ball, *Slaves in the Family*, 236.

30. Lambert, *SC Loyalists*, 266, 280, 292; Anne S. Deas, *Recollections of the Ball Family of South Carolina and The Comingtee Plantation* (Charleston: South Carolina Historical Society, 1978), 102–6; Ball, *Slaves in the* Family, 237.

31. Lambert, *SC Loyalists*, 186, 294.

Terror and Death in the Delta

1. Timothy J. Lockley, ed., *Maroon Communities in South Carolina* (Columbia: University of South Carolina Press, 2009), 98.

2. Lockley, 96.

3. Lockley, 96, 104.

4. Lockley, 99–104.

5. Lockley, 129.

6. Douglas R. Egerton, *He Shall Go Out Free: The Lives of Denmark Vesey* (Lanham, MD: Rowman & Littlefield, 2004), 42; George C. Rogers, Jr., *The History of Georgetown County, South Carolina* (Columbia: University of South Carolina Press, 1970), 343; Walter Edgar, *South Carolina: A History* (Columbia: University of South Carolina Press, 1998), 330; William R. Ryan, *The World of Thomas Jeremiah: Charles Town on the Eve of the American Revolution* (New York: Oxford University Press, 2010), 111.

7. Egerton, *He Shall Go Out Free*, 183; Douglas R. Egerton and Robert L. Paquette, *The Denmark Vesey Affair: A Documentary History* (Gainesville: University Press of Florida, 2017), 76–80, 391, 438.

8. Egerton, *He Shall Go Out Free,* 203–4, 215–21; Steven A. Channing, *Crisis of Fear: Secession in South Carolina* (New York: Simon and Schuster, 1970), 50.

9. Edgar, *South Carolina*, p. 327; Egerton, *He Shall Go Out Free*, 203–5, 209.

10. Egerton, 32–33, 213.

11. Ira Berlin, *Many Thousands Gone: The First Two Centuries of Slavery in North America* (Cambridge, MA: Harvard University Press, 1998), 98, 306; John Hope Franklin and Loren Schweninger, *Runaway Slaves: Rebels on the Plantation* (New York: Oxford University Press, 1999), 291–93.

12. "Shipwreck," *Charleston Courier*, October 9, 1822.

13. Excerpt from *Gallatin* log, *Charleston Courier*, October 2, 1822.

14. *Charleston Courier,* October 1, 1822.

15. Excerpt from letter from North Santee, *Charleston Courier*, October 4, 1822.

16. *Charleston Courier*, October 4, 1822; Anne B. L. Bridges and Roy Williams III, *St. James Santee Plantation Parish: History and Records, 1685–1925* (Spartanburg, SC: Reprint Company, 1997), 166–67.

17. Edgar, *South Carolina*, 285; Elias B. Bull, "Storm Towers of the Santee Delta," *South Carolina Historical Magazine* 81, no. 2 (1980): 101; David Doar, *Rice and Rice Plantings in the South Carolina Low Country*. Contributions from the Charleston Museum, no. 8 (Charleston: Charleston Museum, 1936), 22; Bill Mace, interview with Bob Raynor, December 6, 2015, VSD, 16; John Lane and Philip Wilkinson, *Seven Days on the Santee Delta* (Charleston: Evening Post Books, 2020), 101.

18. Lockley, *Maroon Communities in South Carolina*, 112–13.

19. Lockley, 118; Catherine Clinton, *Harriet Tubman: The Road to Freedom* (New York: Back Bay Books, 2004), 90; George and Willene Hendrick, eds., *Fleeing for Freedom: Stories of the Underground Railroad as Told by Levi Coffin and William Still* (Chicago: Ivan R. Dee, 2004), 7; Frederick Douglass, *Narrative of the Life of Frederick Douglass, an American Slave* (New York: Barnes and Noble Classics, 2003), 69.

Women of Hampton

1. Eliza Lucas Pinckney to Thomas Pinckney (1750–1828), May 17, 1779, in *The Papers of Eliza Lucas Pinckney and Harriot Pinckney Horry Digital Edition* (hereinafter cited as *Pinckney and Horry Papers*), ed. Constance Schulz (Charlottesville: University of Virginia Press, Rotunda, 2012), 2–3, http://rotunda.upress.virginia.edu/PinckneyHorry/ELP0967.

2. Harriott H. Ravenel, *Eliza Pinckney* (New York: Scribner, 1896. Reprinted with the "Journal and Letters of Eliza Lucas," Spartanburg, SC: Reprint Company, 1967), 276–77; Eliza Lucas Pinckney to Thomas Pinckney, *Pinckney and Horry Papers*, May 17, 1779, 3.

3. Ravenel, *Eliza Pinckney*, 274.

4. "Middleton of South Carolina," *South Carolina Historical and Genealogical Magazine* 1, no. 3 (1900): 228–62, http://www.jstor.org/stable/27574919; Constance B. Schulz, "Eliza Lucas Pinckney and Harriott Pinckney Horry: A South Carolina Revolutionary-Era Mother and Daughter," in *South Carolina Women: Their Lives and Times*, vol. 1, ed. Marjorie J. Spruill, Valinda W. Littlefield, and Joan M. Johnson (Athens: University of Georgia Press, 2009), 97–98.

5. Charles Cotesworth Pinckney (1746–1825) was the first son of Charles and Eliza Pinckney. He was educated in England, and became a proponent of the American colony's cause before his return. He served in the 1775 Provincial Congress, and had various military roles in the Revolutionary War, including being an aide-de-camp to Washington in 1777–78. He commanded a regiment that attacked Savannah, and then defended Charleston. At its fall he was held as a prisoner of war first at Snee Farm, and then on parole in Philadelphia. He returned to his practice of law after the war, and in 1787 was a delegate to the Philadelphia Constitutional Convention. Washington appointed Pinckney to be minister to France in 1796. He continued a career in politics as a Federalist, and had unsuccessful campaigns for vice-president in 1800; and twice for president in 1804 and 1808. Biographical sketches, in *Pinckney and Horry Papers*, 5–7.

6. Arthur M. Middleton (1742–1787) was educated in England, and after his return was elected in 1765 to the Commons House of Assembly. He returned to Europe for three years, and upon his return in 1772 was elected again to the Assembly, and then in 1774 to the Provincial Congress. He was a delegate to the Continental Congress, and signed the Declaration of Independence. He served in the defense of Charleston, and as a prisoner of war was held in St. Augustine; his estate including Middleton Place was sequestered. He was exchanged in 1781 and appointed to Congress, and reelected in 1782. "Middleton of South Carolina," *South Carolina Historical and Genealogical Magazine* 1, no. 3 (1900): 242–45, http://www.jstor.org/stable/27574919.

7. Edward Rutledge (1749–1800) was educated in Charleston and England. He and his oldest brother John in 1774 were elected as delegates to the Continental Congress, the next year to the Provincial Congress, and re-elected again in 1776. He was a signer of the Declaration of Independence. His military service in the Revolutionary War included as an artillery captain in the militia. He was imprisoned by the British at St. Augustine. He was exchanged in 1781, and elected to the SC House of Representatives where he served a number of terms. He was elected to become South Carolina Governor in 1798. Mabel L. Webber, "Dr. John Rutledge and His Descendants," *South Carolina Historical and Genealogical Magazine* 31, no. 1 (1930): 22–24, http://www.jstor.org/stable/27569816.

8. Charles Drayton Sr. (1743–1822) along with his brother was educated in England. Upon his return to Carolina in 1771, his allegiance swung from the Crown to colonial resistance. His marriage to Hester Middleton placed him in a family with a high degree of passion for the revolutionary cause. He became a captain of an artillery regiment, and upon the fall of Charleston, Drayton signed the petition giving him protection, and retreated to his property at Goose Creek. After the war's end, he was able to escape confiscation of his properties, including Drayton Hall. Dorothy Griffin, "The Eighteenth-Century Draytons of Drayton Hall," (PhD diss., Emory University, 1985), 333–43.

9. Henry Middleton (1717–1784) inherited extensive properties from his father in England, Barbados, and Carolina. He became involved in politics in the colony, first as a member and then Speaker of the Assembly, and then the Royal Council. He resigned that seat to align himself with the cause of liberty, serving in the Continental Congress including a time as president. In 1775 he became president of the Provincial Congress, and due to illness did not return to the Continental Congress, his son Arthur taking his place. At the fall of Charleston, he retired to his planation The Oaks, and accepted the re-establishment of British rule. "Middleton of South Carolina," *South Carolina Historical and Genealogical Magazine* 1, no. 3 (1900): 239–40, http://www.jstor.org/stable/27574919; Edward McCrady, *The History of South Carolina in the Revolution, 1775–1780* (New York: Russell & Russell, 1901), 535.

10. Ralph Izard (1742–1804) was educated in England. He married the niece of the governor of New York, and returned to Europe, establishing a residence in England, and traveled on the Continent. The conflict with the colonies precipitated a move to Paris, where he was involved in negotiations with France. Upon returning to Philadelphia, he became a delegate from South Carolina to the Continental Congress. After the war he became a U.S. senator. "Izard of South Carolina," *South Carolina Historical and Genealogical Magazine* 2, no. 3 (1901): 214–17, http://www.jstor.org/stable/27574958.

11. John Mathews (1744–1802) studied law in England. He began his political life in 1767 when elected to the Assembly. He was also elected to the first and second Provincial Congresses in 1775, and served on eight General Assemblies before his election to the Continental Congress in 1778, and re-election in 1779 and 1780. He left that Congress, and upon his return to SC in 1781 he joined the legislature and the next year was elected governor. He served in that office only a year, and returned to his work with the legislature. Walter Edgar, ed., *The South Carolina Encyclopedia* (Columbia: University of South Carolina Press, 2006), 598–99.

12. Daniel Huger (1741–1799) was born at Limerick Plantation on the Cooper River, and received his secondary education in England. He won a seat on the Second General Assembly, and then was reelected for the Third. He was also elected to the Privy Council. Prior to the fall of Charleston, he evacuated with Governor John Rutledge to enable the civil government to continue, but later changed directions and returned to the city to accept British protection. Somehow he was able to avoid confiscation or amercement of his properties. He had an estate on the Wateree River and a town house in Charleston, and won further elections, including to the first and second U.S. Congresses. In 1785 he fought a duel and wounded Charles Cotesworth Pinckney. Walter B. Edgar and N. Louise Bailey, eds., *Biographical Directory of the South Carolina House of Representatives, the Commons House of Assembly, 1692–1775* (Columbia: University of South Carolina Press, 1977), II: 340–41.

13. William Henry Drayton (1742–1779) was the son of John Drayton and Charlotta Bull (daughter of Lieutenant Governor William Bull.) He and his brother Charles traveled with the Pinckneys to England for their education. He was recalled by his father to Carolina before completing his degree. In 1765 he won a seat in the Royal Assembly but lost it in the next election. His pro-England views earned him enmity in the colony, and he returned to live in England. His initial allegiance won him a place on the Provincial Council in Charleston. Ongoing frustrations with the Crown's actions and policies turned him toward the colony's side, so much that he was stripped of his Council seat in 1775. Instead he was elected to the Provincial Congress. His efforts and writings earned him a seat in the 1778 Continental

Congress. Walter Edgar, ed., *The South Carolina Encyclopedia* (Columbia: University of South Carolina Press, 2006), 274–75.

14. Thomas Pinckney (1750–1828) was educated in England, and like his brother Charles Cotesworth was aligned with the American cause. He became an officer in the First South Carolina Continental Regiment, and participated in the attack on Savannah and the defense of Charleston. He escaped the city prior to its capture, and joined in the Battle of Camden, where he experienced a compound leg fracture, and was imprisoned. Pinckney went on to serve in the South Carolina House of Representatives, and then governor from 1787 to 1789. He was president of the state convention ratifying the US Constitution. President Washington appointed him as US minister to Great Britain in 1792, and then on a special mission to Spain, where he negotiated the 1795 Treaty of San Lorenzo. Biographical sketches, in *Pinckney and Horry Papers*, 7–8.

15. Ravenel, *Eliza Pinckney*, 274.

16. Biographical sketches, in *Pinckney and Horry Papers*, 2–3.

17. Keith Krawczynski, *William Henry Drayton: South Carolina Revolutionary Patriot* (Baton Rouge: Louisiana State University Press, 2001), 9; Emily Taylor, "The Draytons of South Carolina and Philadelphia," *Genealogical Society of Pennsylvania* 8, no. 1 (March 1921), 9–10.

18. Biographical sketches, in *Pinckney and Horry Papers*, 2–3.

19. Schulz, "Eliza Lucas Pinckney," 79; Darcy R. Fryer, "The Mind of Eliza Pinckney: An Eighteenth-Century Woman's Construction of Herself," *South Carolina Historical Magazine* 99, no. 3 (1998): 215–37, http://www.jstor.org/stable/27570314.

20. Biographical sketches, in *Pinckney and Horry Papers*, 1–2; Walter Edgar, *South Carolina: A History* (Columbia: University of South Carolina Press, 1998), 146; Fryer, "The Mind of Eliza Pinckney," 217; Schulz, "Eliza Lucas Pinckney," 79.

21. Elise Pinckney, ed., *The Letterbook of Eliza Lucas Pinckney, 1739–1762* (Chapel Hill: University of North Carolina Press, 1972; repr., Columbia: University of South Carolina Press, 1997), 32–33, 34–35, 38, 41.

22. Pinckney, ed., *The Letterbook of Eliza Lucas Pinckney*, 51–54, 167; Schulz, "Eliza Lucas Pinckney," 95; Ravenel, *Eliza Pinckney*, 115–18; Eliza Lucas Pinckney to Thomas Pinckney, August 1780, in *Pinckney and Horry Papers*.

23. Fryer, "The Mind of Eliza Pinckney," 232–33; Schulz, "Eliza Lucas Pinckney," 103–5.

24. Schulz, "Eliza Lucas Pinckney," 97.

25. Daniel Huger Horry, Jr., Inventory, January 16, 1786, in *Pinckney and Horry Papers*.

26. Charles Joyner, *Down by the Riverside: A South Carolina Slave Community* (Urbana: University of Illinois Press, 1984), 62.

27. Leland Ferguson, *Uncommon Ground: Archaeology and Early African America, 1650–1800* (Washington, DC: Smithsonian Institution Press, 1992), xxxv–xxxix, 123.

28. Stacey L. Young, "The Hampton Plantation Community Project," report prepared for South Carolina Department of State Parks, Recreation and Tourism, Hampton Plantation State Historic Site Resource Management (January 2014), 10.

29. Young, 67–71.

30. Susan B. Bates and Harriott C. Leland, *French Santee: A Huguenot Settlement in Colonial South Carolina* (Baltimore: Otter Bay Books, 2015), 182.

31. T. Benton Young, "Sue Alston: Angel of Hampton Plantation," *Carolana* 2, no. 7 (July 1985): 10, 36, 38.

32. Young, "Sue Alston," 10.

33. Gerald Alston, interview with Bob Raynor, November 23, 2015, VSD, 9; Henrietta Smalls, interview with Bob Raynor, March 14, 2016, VSD, 13–15.

34. Jim Fulcher, personal communication with author, November 6, 2019.

35. Archibald Rutledge, *God's Children* (Charleston: History Press: 2009), 46.

36. Sue Alston, interview with John Egerton, August 25, 1976, John Egerton Papers, Special Collections, Jean and Alexander Heard Library, Vanderbilt University.

Tale of the Two Great Canoeists

1. Geoffrey Wolff, *The Hard Way Around: The Passages of Joshua Slocum* (New York: Alfred A. Knopf, 2010), 8, 10.

2. Nathaniel H. Bishop, *Voyage of the Paper Canoe* (Santa Barbara, CA: Narrative Press, 2001), 153.

3. Bishop, 196.

4. Bishop, 198.

5. Joshua Slocum, *Sailing Alone Around the World, and Voyage of the Liberdade* (London: Rupert Hart-Davis Ltd., 1948), 31.

6. Slocum, 375–76.

7. Slocum, 383.

Swimming the Santee

1. Ball, Charles Ball, *Slavery in the United States: A Narrative of the Life and Adventures of Charles Ball, a Black Man* (New York: Negro Universities Press, 1969), 392–93, 415, 421, 423.

2. Anne B. L. Bridges, and Roy Williams III, *St. James Santee Plantation Parish: History and Records, 1685–1925* (Spartanburg, SC: Reprint Company, 1997), 75–77.

3. Harriott H. Ravenel, *Eliza Pinckney* (New York: Scribner, 1896. Reprinted with the "Journal and Letters of Eliza Lucas," Spartanburg, SC: Reprint Company, 1967), 284–85.

4. John Lane and Philip Wilkinson, *Seven Days on the Santee Delta* (Charleston: Evening Post Books, 2020), 114–15.

5. Phil Wilkinson, interview with Bob Raynor, January 25, 2016, VSD, 32–35.

6. Henry H. Carter, *Early History of the Santee Club* (Self-published, 1934), 6–7.

7. William Garrett, interview with Bob Raynor, June 14, 2016, VSD, 5–6.

8. Archibald Rutledge, *Home by the River* (Orangeburg, SC: Sandlapper Publishing Inc., copyright 1941 by the Bobbs-Merrill Company), 131.

They Changed the River

1. Pat Ferris, pre-interview discussion with Bob Raynor, October 2015, VSD.

2. Mark Kinzer, *Nature's Return: An Environmental History of Congaree National Park* (Columbia: University of South Carolina Press, 2017), 88.

3. Archibald Rutledge, *Home by the River* (New York: Bobbs-Merrill Company, 1941), 130, 137.

4. Henry Savage, Jr., *River of the Carolinas: The Santee* (New York: Rinehart & Company, 1956), 346–49.

5. Hart, T. Robert, "The Lowcountry Landscape: Politics, Preservation, and the Santee-Cooper Project," *Environmental History* 18, no. 1 (January 2013): 138, http://www.jstor.org/stable/41721484; Jack Irby Hayes, Jr., *South Carolina and the New Deal* (Columbia: University of South Carolina Press, 2001), 75–78.

6. Hayes, 80–81.

7. Hayes, 81.

8. Alexander Sprunt, Jr. and E. Burnham Chamberlain, *South Carolina Bird Life*, revised edition, with a supplement, E. Milby Burton (Columbia: University of South Carolina Press, 1970), 340–41.

9. Hart, "Lowcountry Landscape," 141–42, 149–50; Matthew Lockhart, "From Rice Fields to Duck Marshes: Sport Hunters and Environmental Change on the South Carolina Coast, 1890–1950," (PhD diss., University of South Carolina, 2017), 353, ProQuest (10266277); Hayes, *South Carolina*, 82.

10. Hayes, *South Carolina*, 83–84; Walter B. Edgar, *History of Santee Cooper 1934–1984* (Columbia: R. L. Bryan, 1984), 10.

11. Hart, "Lowcountry Landscape," 144; Archibald Rutledge, "Dam Everything," *Field and Stream* (November 1947): 38, 116.

12. Pat Ferris, interview by Bob Raynor, November 6, 2015, VSD, 15.

13. Lockhart, "From Rice Fields to Duck Marshes," 374–76.

14. Leroy M. Want, "Harm to Santee Lands Is Charged," *Charleston News and Courier*, February 3, 1942, 1–2.

15. Santee Basin Diadromous Fish Restoration Plan, National Marine Fisheries Service (NMFS), North Carolina Wildlife Resources Commission (NMFC), South Carolina Department of Natural Resources (SCDNR), U.S. Fish and Wildlife Service (FWS), 2017, 32, https://www.dnr.sc.gov/fish/pdf/SanteeBasinDiadromousFishRestorationPlan.pdf; Björn Kjerfve and J. E. Greer, "Hydrography of the Santee River During Moderate Discharge Conditions," *Estuaries* 1, no. 2 (June 1978): 111.

16. Allyson Bird, "Turning the Tides: State, Federal Agencies Celebrate 25th Anniversary of Powerhouse Project," *Charleston Post and Courier*, March 26, 2010, B1; Fred Rigsbee, "Cooper River Rediversion Project Correcting 40-Year-Old Mistake," *Charleston News and Courier*, March 19, 1989, 6; Kjerfve, "Hydrography," 118.

17. Bob Baldwin, personal communication with the author, 2007.

18. Lockhart, "From Rice Fields to Duck Marshes," 310–12; Brenda L. Hockensmith, "Flow and Salinity Characteristics of the Santee River Estuary, South Carolina," South Carolina Department of Natural Resources, 2004; Bill Mace, personal communication with the author, September 2019.

19. Santee Basin Diadromous Fish Restoration Plan, 6.

20. South Carolina Department of Natural Resources, "History of the St. Stephen Fish Lift," http://dnr.sc.gov/timelinestephen/.

21. Santee Basin Diadromous Fish Restoration Plan, 6, 66.

22. William R. Lowry, *Dam Politics: Restoring America's Rivers* (Washington: Georgetown University Press, 2003), 4; Björn Kjerfve, "The Santee-Cooper: A Study of Estuarine Manipulations," in *Estuarine Processes: Uses, Stresses, and Adaptation to the Estuary*, vol. 1, ed. Martin Wiley (New York: Academic Press, 1976), 54.

Protecting the Delta

1. Richard D. Porcher, Jr., and William R. Judd, *The Market Preparation of Carolina Rice: An Illustrated History of Innovations in the Lowcountry Rice Kingdom* (Columbia: University of South Carolina Press, 2014), 299–300.

2. Matthew Lockhart, "From Rice Fields to Duck Marshes: Sport Hunters and Environmental Change on the South Carolina Coast, 1890–1950," (PhD diss., University of South Carolina, 2017), 76–77, ProQuest (10266277).

3. Lockhart, 172, 251; Phil Wilkinson, interview with Bob Raynor, January 25, 2016, VSD, 26–27.

4. Henry H. Carter, *Early History of the Santee Club* (self-published, 1934), 3–4; William Garrett, interview with Bob Raynor, June 14, 2016, VSD, 8–10.

5. Lockhart, 375–76.

6. Bill Birchard, *Nature's Keepers* (San Francisco: Jossey-Bass, 2005), 41–42; *Tom Yawkey Wildlife Center* (Columbia: South Carolina Department of Natural Resources, 1979), 5.

7. Peter Matthiessen, "Happy Days," *Audubon* 77, no. 6 (November 1975): 64.

8. William Garrett, interview with Bob Raynor, June 14, 2016, VSD, 18.

9. Matthiessen, "Happy Days," 93.

10. Greg Lucas, "At Home in Eden," *South Carolina Wildlife* (November/December 2000): 10-11.

11. Tony Bartelme and Glenn Smith, "The Secret Delta," *Post and Courier* (September 15, 2019); Kenny Williams, interview with Bob Raynor, December 7, 2016, VSD, 13.

12. Mike Prevost, interview with Bob Raynor, September 18, 2016, VSD, 12; T. Edward Nickens, "The Wild Santee," *Garden and Gun* (October/November 2016), 121; Pierre Manigault, interview with Bob Raynor, February 1, 2016, VSD, 8–9; John H. Tibbetts, "The Bird Chase," *Coastal Heritage* 15, no. 4 (spring 2001): 13.

13. *St. James Santee: The Brick Church at Wambaw*, St. James Santee Brick Church Restoration Committee (Charleston: Wyrick & Company, 2003), 78–85.

14. Phil Wilkinson, interview with Bob Raynor, January 25, 2016, VSD, 2; Anne B. L. Bridges and Roy Williams III, *St. James Santee Plantation Parish: History and Records, 1685–1925* (Spartanburg, SC: Reprint Company, 1997), 127–28.

15. Suzanne C. Linder and Marta L. Thacker, *Historical Atlas of the Rice Plantations of Georgetown County and the Santee River* (Columbia: South Carolina Department of Archives and History for the Historic Ricefields Association, 2001), 758–59.

16. Phil Wilkinson, interview with Bob Raynor, January 25, 2016, VSD, 6, 50; Pat Ferris, interview with Bob Raynor, November 6, 2015, VSD, 4.

Epilogue

1. Anne B. L. Bridges, and Roy Williams III, *St. James Santee Plantation Parish: History and Records, 1685–1925* (Spartanburg, SC: Reprint Company, 1997), 59; Suzanne C. Linder and Marta L. Thacker, *Historical Atlas of the Rice Plantations of Georgetown County and the Santee River* (Columbia: South Carolina Department of Archives and History for the Historic Ricefields Association, 2001), 673.

2. George C. Rogers, Jr., *The History of Georgetown County, South Carolina* (Columbia: University of South Carolina Press, 1970), 201, 228–29 n16; Allan Charles, "Visitors' Views of South Carolina Roads Before 1833," *Carologue* 11, no. 1 (Spring 1996), 12.

3. Phil Wilkinson, interview with Bob Raynor, January 25, 2016, VSD, 28.

4. Jane Wineglass, interview with Bob Raynor, December 14, 2015, VSD.

5. Stephanie Waldron, interview with Bob Raynor, June 27, 2016, VSD; letter of Richard Dominick to Mr. Bishop, June 10, 1975, South Carolina Historical Society.

6. Charles Joyner, *Down by the Riverside: A South Carolina Slave Community* (Urbana: University of Illinois Press, 1984), 43.

Acknowledgments

I am grateful for the valuable help I received from numerous librarians and archivists in Charleston, the Lowcountry, and beyond. The Charleston County Public Library, and particularly the South Carolina Room in the downtown library, was a tremendous resource, and I appreciate the help from Charlotte Smith, Tish Thompson, and Marianne Cawley. The interlibrary loan division allowed me to put my hand on sources not available locally. The encouragement of Nic Butler, public historian for the library, was appreciated. The South Carolina Historical Society's Special Collections staff was also most helpful, especially librarian Molly Silliman. Virginia Ellison and Lauren Nivens of SCHS were always responsive in my tracking down items in the archives. At the Village Museum in McClellanville, Bud Hill went out of his way to share pertinent resources. The Ocean County Library in New Jersey was receptive to my exploring the archive of the paper canoeist, Nathaniel Holmes Bishop, particularly librarian Colleen Goode. Cheves Leland allowed me to peruse the plats in the archives of the Huguenot Society of South Carolina. Brenda Burk at the Clemson University Special Collections and Archives helped me track down an illustration. Al Hester, Historic Sites Coordinator for the State Park Service, was generous in sharing historical resources of Hampton Plantation. Richard Porcher and William Judd were also generous in offering illustrations from *Market Preparation of Rice*, as was Bill Post of the South Carolina Department of Natural Resources (SCDNR) for sharing a map of the Santee Basin.

My interest in hearing from the people of the Santee Delta evolved into an oral history project – *Voices of the Santee Delta*. The CEO of the South Carolina Historical Society, Faye Jensen, believed in the project, and gave her personal and institutional support. The co-sponsoring organization, the Village Museum, was integrally involved with Bud Hill as the project's director. I received assistance in identifying and making contact with potential interviewees from Sheila Powell, Marcella Smalls, Bill Mace, and Mike Prevost. But I am most appreciative of the people, the *Voices of the Santee Delta*, who participated in the interviews with me: Gerald Alston, Pat Ferris, William Garrett, Bill Mace, Pierre Manigault, Mike Prevost, Henrietta Smalls, Stephanie Waldron, Phil Wilkinson, Kenny Williams, and Jane Wineglass. At the time of this writing, Mrs. Smalls, Mrs. Wineglass, Mr. Ferris, and Mr. Garrett had passed away.

Various people facilitated my trips and experiences in the Santee Delta. I traveled to Murphy Island initially with the invitation of Jim Westerhold of SCDNR and with Bill Mace, a few years later with John Dupree, and again with Chris Crolley. Chris also lent his fine canoe for a three-day trip I made with accomplished paddler Ian Sanchez to Murphy and Cedar Islands, and Ian's expertise and companionship on this trip was invaluable. I also received an invitation to participate in a public archaeology project at Hampton Plantation State Historic Site from Vennie Deas-Moore, and was welcomed by archaeologists Martha Zierden, Stacey Young, and David Jones. Alexander Lofton was gracious in allowing my visit to his property, Wambaw Plantation (Horry/Lucas).

Besides the ready reference of Richard Porcher's written work, he also was available for natural history inquiries, and like many other people in the Lowcountry, I have benefitted from accompanying him on field trips. John Brubaker was additionally a natural history resource. Billy Baldwin has been a constant source of encouragement for my writing, and years ago informed me of the "paper canoeist". Another Baldwin from McClellanville, Bob, shared information as I worked on *Tracing the Cape Romain Archipelago*, and I revisited this interview for his insights about the changing water chemistry of the Santee Delta after Rediversion.

For reviewing chapters, I would like to thank Gary McGee, Ginny Prevost, Al Hester, Bud Hill, Bob Morgan, Mike Prevost, and Ted Rosengarten; Ted's feedback made the overall book better. Bob Morgan engaged in the search for the Ball Wambaw Plantation in the last year of his employment with Francis Marion

National Forest, and saw this effort to success. Jim and Patty Fulcher were kind to recount their interactions with Sue Alston.

I would like to thank Michael Nolan for his support of bringing this work to publication with Evening Post Books, and I also appreciate the assistance of Elizabeth Hollerith. The fine look of the book both inside and out is the skilled design work of Aren Staiger. Gretchen Dykstra did a thorough job of the copyediting.

As in the past, I appreciated the counsel of Steve Hoffius. Besides the specific help mentioned above from the Prevosts, both Ginny and Mike were constant sources of encouragement. My wife Susan was most supportive and understanding of my multiple trips to the Santee Delta, and my focus on this lengthy project.

I exonerate all those listed above for the book's content; I am solely responsible for any errors.

Illustration Credits

Cover

Sunrise on the Santee Delta, photograph by author, 2014; Charleston District, South Carolina. Robert Mills, Atlas of the State of South Carolina, 1825. Courtesy of the Library of Congress.

End pages

Charleston District, and Georgetown District, South Carolina. Robert Mills, Atlas of the State of South Carolina, 1825. Courtesy of the Library of Congress.

Prologue

Page iv   Santee River Coast Survey 1875. From the collections of the South Carolina Historical Society.

Page 2   The Santee River basin. Courtesy of SCDNR/NOAA.

The Prehistoric Delta

Page 6   Swamp forest in Audubon's Beidler Forest Sanctuary, photograph by author, 2020.

Page 11   Along the Intracoastal Waterway at archaeological site 38GE46, photograph by author, 2011.

The Command of Water

Page 17   Felling a tree in the Santee Swamp (Box 21, folder 2006.028, P-2467); from the Visual Materials Discrete Collection, 1850 – 2016, at the South Carolina Historical Society. Photograph by W. Lincoln Highton, 1940, Photographic Section, Information Division. Federal Works Agency, Washington, D.C.

Page 19   Operation of a tide trunk. Reproduced by permission from Richard Dwight Porcher, Jr., and William Robert Judd, *The Market Preparation of Carolina Rice*, 74.

Page 20   Rice trunk and impoundment in the Santee Delta. From the collections of the South Carolina Historical Society.

Page 23   Rice harvest on Annandale 1921 (27023KGC). Courtesy of the Kinloch Gun Club Collection, Georgetown County Library, Georgetown, South Carolina.

Page 26   Moving the rice trunk (27089KGC). Courtesy of the Kinloch Gun Club Collection, Georgetown County Library, Georgetown, South Carolina.

Wambaw

Page 37   Wambaw Creek, photograph by author, 2016.

Page 44   Plat of Wambaw Creek land (32-39-06); from the Maps/Plats collections at the South Carolina Historical Society. Joseph Purcell, 1795.

Terror and Death in the Delta

Page 53   Negroes hiding in the swamps of Louisiana. William Ludwell Sheppard, artist; James L. Langridge, engraver. Courtesy of the Library of Congress.

Page 57   Impoundment on Murphy Island, photograph by author, 2014.

Page 59   Murphy Island storm tower, photograph by author, 2014.

Women of Hampton

Page 64   The Hampton mansion, Hampton Plantation State Historic Site, photograph by author, 2012.

Page 71   Site of slave dwelling, Hampton Plantation State Historic Site, photograph by author, 2015.

Page 74   Chimney remains of Prince and Sue Alston's house, Hampton Plantation State Historic Site, photograph by author, 2021.

Tale of the Two Great Canoeists

Page 79   Ian Sanchez in canoe, photograph by author, 2014.

Page 81   Home of the Alligator, frontispiece in *The Voyage of the Paper Canoe* (Edinburgh: David Douglas, 1878), illustrations by Waud and Merrill, engraved by John Andrew and Son.

Page 83   Joshua Slocum, wife, and two children aboard *Liberdade*. Courtesy of the New Bedford Whaling Museum.

Swimming the Santee

Page 89   The South Santee River along the Santee Coastal Reserve, photograph by author, 2014.

They Changed the River

Page 92   Map of Santee-Cooper Project, n.d., Poe Family Papers, Clemson University Special Collections and Archives, oversize folder 1, Clemson University Libraries, Clemson, SC.

Page 95   From the SCHS Visual Materials Discrete Collection, 1850 – 2016 (Box 21, folder 2006.028, P-2468) at the South Carolina Historical Society. Photograph by W. Lincoln Highton, 1940. Photographic Section, Information Division. Federal Works Agency, Washington, D.C.

Page 96   From the SCHS Visual Materials Discrete Collection, 1850 – 2016 (Box 2, folder 2000.031) at the South Carolina Historical Society. Photography by Thompson, 1941.

Protecting the Delta

Page 104   One of the managed impoundments in the Santee Delta Wildlife Management Area, photograph by author, 2015.

Page 106   Jimmy Singleton and an unidentified employee place duck decoys in the water near Kinloch Plantation, (27015KGC). Courtesy of the Kinloch Gun Club Collection, Georgetown County Library, Georgetown, South Carolina.

Page 107   The Santee Gun Clubhouse, photograph by author, 2013.

Page 111   Impounded waters of the Washo Reserve, photograph by author, 2013.

Page 116   East portico column, Brick Church (Wambaw Church), photograph by author, 2020.

Epilogue

Page 122   Swamp forest in Congaree National Park, photograph by author, 2020.

Page 124   Swamp forest in Audubon's Beidler Forest Sanctuary, photograph by author, 2020.

Page 127   Santee Delta Wildlife Management Area, photograph by author, 2020.

Page 132   Jane Wineglass, photograph by author, 2015.

BIBLIOGRAPHY

Alston, J. Motte. *Rice Planter and Sportsman: The Recollections of J. Motte Alston, 1821–1909*. Edited by Arney R. Childs. Columbia: University of South Carolina Press, 1953.

Alston, Sue, interviewed with John Egerton, August 25, 1976. John Egerton Papers, Special Collections, The Jean and Alexander Heard Library, Vanderbilt University.

Ball, Charles. *Slavery in the United States: A Narrative of the Life and Adventures of Charles Ball, a Black Man*. New York: Negro Universities Press, 1969. First published in 1837.

Ball, Edward. *Slaves in the Family*. New York: Farrar, Straus and Giroux, 1998.

Bartram, John, and Francis Harper. "Diary of a Journey through the Carolinas, Georgia, and Florida, from July 1, 1765, to April 10, 1766." *Transactions of the American Philosophical Society*, n.s., 33, no. 1, Philadelphia (1942), i–iv, 1–120.

Bartram, William. *The Travels of William Bartram: Naturalist's Edition*. Edited with commentary and an annotated index by Francis Harper. Athens: University of Georgia Press, 1998.

Bass, Robert D. *Swamp Fox: The Life and Campaigns of General Francis Marion.* Orangeburg, SC: Sandlapper Publishing, 1974.

Bates, Susan B., and Harriott C. Leland. *French Santee: A Huguenot Settlement in Colonial South Carolina.* Baltimore: Otter Bay Books, 2015.

Beach, Virginia C. *Rice & Ducks: The Surprising Convergence that Saved the Carolina Lowcountry.* Charleston: Evening Post Books, 2014.

Berlin, Ira. *Many Thousands Gone: The First Two Centuries of Slavery in North America.* Cambridge, MA: Harvard University Press, 1998.

Birchard, Bill. *Nature's Keepers.* San Francisco: Jossey-Bass, 2005.

Bishop, Nathaniel H. *Voyage of the Paper Canoe.* Santa Barbara, CA: Narrative Press, 2001. First published in 1878.

Booker, Karen, Charles Hudson, and Robert Rankin. "Place Name Identification and Multilingualism in the Sixteenth-Century Southeast." *Ethnohistory* 39 (1992): 399–451.

Bridges, Anne B. L., and Roy Williams III. *St. James Santee Plantation Parish: History and Records, 1685-1925.* Spartanburg, SC: Reprint Company, 1997.

Bull, Elias B. "Storm Towers of the Santee Delta." *South Carolina Historical Magazine* 81, no. 2 (1980): 95–101.

Carney, Judith. *Black Rice.* Cambridge, MA: Harvard University Press, 2001.

Carter, Henry H. *Early History of the Santee Club.* Self-published: 1934.

Channing, Steven A. *Crisis of Fear: Secession in South Carolina.* New York: Simon and Schuster, 1970.

Charles, Allan. "Visitors' Views of South Carolina Roads Before 1833." *Carologue* 11, no. 1 (Spring 1996): 11–12.

Clinton, Catherine. *Harriet Tubman: The Road to Freedom.* New York: Back Bay Books, 2004.

Deas, Anne S. *Recollections of the Ball Family of South Carolina and The Comingtee Plantation.* Charleston: South Carolina Historical Society, 1978. Reprint of 1909 edition.

Dennis, John. *The Great Cypress Swamps.* Baton Rouge: Louisiana State University Press, 1988.

DePratter, Chester. "Cofitachequi." In *The Forgotten Centuries: Indians and Europeans in the American South, 1521–1704*, edited by Charles Hudson and Carmen Tesser. Athens: University of Georgia Press, 1994.

DePratter, Chester, and Val Green. "John Lawson and the Great Catawba Trading Path." *Carologue* (Autumn 2000), 16–20.

Doar, David. *Rice and Rice Plantings in the South Carolina Low Country*. Contributions from the Charleston Museum, no. 8. Charleston: Charleston Museum, 1936.

Douglass, Frederick. *Narrative of the Life of Frederick Douglass, an American Slave*. New York: Barnes and Noble Classics, 2003.

Dubois, Laurent. *Avengers of the New World: The Story of the Haitian Revolution*. Cambridge, MA: Harvard University Press, 2004.

Dubose, Samuel, and Frederick A. Porcher. *A Contribution to the History of the Huguenots of South Carolina, Consisting of Pamphlets*. Edited by Theodore G. Thomas. New York: Knickerbocker Press, 1887.

Edelson, S. Max. *Plantation Enterprise in Colonial South Carolina*. Cambridge, MA: Harvard University Press, 2006.

Edgar, Walter B. *History of Santee Cooper 1934–1984*. Columbia: R. L. Bryan, 1984.

Edgar, Walter, ed. *The South Carolina Encyclopedia*. Columbia: University of South Carolina Press, 2006.

Edgar, Walter. *South Carolina: A History*. Columbia: University of South Carolina Press, 1998.

Edgar, Walter B., and N. Louise Bailey, eds. *Biographical Directory of the South Carolina House of Representatives, Vol. 2, the Commons House of Assembly, 1692–1775*. Columbia: University of South Carolina Press, 1977.

Egerton, Douglas R. *He Shall Go Out Free: The Lives of Denmark Vesey*. Lanham, MD: Rowman & Littlefield, 2004.

Egerton, Douglas R., and Robert L. Paquette. *The Denmark Vesey Affair: A Documentary History*. Gainesville: University Press of Florida, 2017.

Espenshade, Christopher T., and Paul E. Brockington, Jr. "An Archaeological Study of the Minim Island Site: Early Woodland Dynamics in Coastal South Carolina." Report by Brockington and Associates, 1989. (tDAR id: 391068); doi:10.6067/XCV80C4WM2.

Ferguson, Leland. *Uncommon Ground: Archaeology and Early African America, 1650–1800*. Washington, DC: Smithsonian Institution Press, 1992.

Fleetwood, William C. Jr. *Tidecraft: The Boats of South Carolina, Georgia and Northeastern Florida, 1550–1950.* Tybee Island, GA: WBG Marine Press, 1995.

Fox-Genovese, Elizabeth. *Within the Plantation Household: Black & White Women of the Old South.* Chapel Hill: University of North Carolina Press, 1988.

Franklin, John H., and Loren Schweninger. *Runaway Slaves: Rebels on the Plantation.* New York: Oxford University Press, 1999.

Fryer, Darcy R. "The Mind of Eliza Pinckney: An Eighteenth-Century Woman's Construction of Herself." *The South Carolina Historical Magazine* 99, no. 3 (1998): 215–37. http://www.jstor.org/stable/27570314.

Gardner, Jeffrey W., and Eric C. Poplin. "Historic Adaptations Through Time: Archaeological Testing of Five Sites, Francis Marion National Forest, Berkeley and Charleston Counties, South Carolina." Report published by Brockington & Associates, 1992. tDAR id: 156118.

Gordon, John W. *South Carolina and the American Revolution: A Battlefield History.* Columbia: University of South Carolina Press, 2003.

Griffin, Dorothy G. "The Eighteenth Century Draytons of Drayton Hall." PhD diss., Emory University, 1985.

Hamer, Philip M., George C. Rogers Jr., C. James Taylor, and David R. Chesnutt, eds., and Peggy J. Clark, ed. asst. *The Papers of Henry Laurens*, 15 vols. Columbia: University of South Carolina Press, 1972–1998.

Harris, Lynn B. *Patroons & Periaguas: Enslaved Watermen and Watercraft of the Lowcountry.* Columbia: University of South Carolina Press, 2014.

Hart, T. Robert. "The Lowcountry Landscape: Politics, Preservation, and the Santee-Cooper Project." *Environmental History* 18, no. 1 (2013): 127–56. http://www.jstor.org/stable/41721484.

Hatfield, April L. "Colonial Southeastern Indian History." *The Journal of Southern History* 73, No. 3 (August 2007), 567–78.

Hayes, Jack Irby, Jr. *South Carolina and the New Deal.* Columbia: University of South Carolina Press, 2001.

Hayes, Miles O., and Jacqueline Michel. *A Coast for all Seasons: A Naturalist's Guide to the Coast of South Carolina.* Columbia: Pandion Books, 2008.

Henderson, Archibald. *Washington's Southern Tour 1791.* Cambridge, MA: The Riverside Press, 1923.

Hendrick, George and Willene, eds. *Fleeing for Freedom: Stories of the Underground Railroad as Told by Levi Coffin and William Still.* Chicago: Ivan R. Dee, 2004.

Hockensmith, Brenda L. "Flow and Salinity Characteristics of the Santee River Estuary, South Carolina." South Carolina Department of Natural Resources, 2004.

"Izard of South Carolina." *The South Carolina Historical and Genealogical Magazine* 2, no. 3 (1901): 205–40. http://www.jstor.org/stable/27574958.

Joyner, Charles. *Down by the Riverside: A South Carolina Slave Community.* Urbana: University of Illinois Press, 1984.

Kinzer, Mark. *Nature's Return: An Environmental History of Congaree National Park.* Columbia: University of South Carolina Press, 2017.

Kjerfve, Björn. "The Santee-Cooper: A Study of Estuarine Manipulations." In *Estuarine Processes: Uses, Stresses, and Adaptation to the Estuary,* ed. Martin Wiley, vol. 1. New York: Academic Press, 1976.

Kjerfve, Björn, and Jeffrey E. Greer, "Hydrography of the Santee River During Moderate Discharge Conditions." *Estuaries* 1, no. 2 (June 1978): 111–19.

Kovacik, Charles, and John Winberry. *South Carolina: A Geography.* Boulder: Westview Press, 1987.

Krawczynski, Keith. *William Henry Drayton: South Carolina Revolutionary Patriot.* Baton Rouge: Louisiana State University Press, 2001.

Lambert, Robert S. *South Carolina Loyalists in the American Revolution.* Columbia: University of South Carolina Press, 1987.

Lane, John, and Philip Wilkinson. *Seven Days on the Santee Delta.* Charleston: Evening Post Books, 2020.

Lawson, John. *A New Voyage to Carolina.* London, 1709.

Linder, Suzanne C., and Marta L. Thacker. *Historical Atlas of the Rice Plantations of Georgetown County and the Santee River.* Columbia: South Carolina Department of Archives and History for the Historic Ricefields Association, 2001.

Littlefield, Daniel C. *Rice and Slaves: Ethnicity and the Slave Trade in Colonial South Carolina.* Urbana: University of Illinois Press, 1981.

Lockhart, Matthew. "From Rice Fields to Duck Marshes: Sport Hunters and Environmental Change on the South Carolina Coast, 1890–1950." PhD diss., University of South Carolina, 2017. ProQuest (10266277).

Lockley, Timothy J., ed. *Maroon Communities in South Carolina.* Columbia: University of South Carolina Press, 2009.

Lowry, William R. *Dam Politics: Restoring America's Rivers.* Washington: Georgetown University Press, 2003.

Lucas, Greg. "At Home in Eden." *South Carolina Wildlife* 47, no. 6 (November/December 2000): 6–15.

Matthiessen, Peter. "Happy Days." *Audubon* 77, no. 6 (November 1975): 64–95.

Mattoon, Wilbur. *The Southern Cypress.* Bulletin No. 272. Washington, U.S. Department of Agriculture, 1915.

McCrady, Edward. *The History of South Carolina in the Revolution 1775–1780.* New York: Russell & Russell, 1901.

McCully, Patrick. *Silenced Rivers: the Ecology and Politics of Large Dams.* London: Zed Books, 1996.

"Middleton of South Carolina." *The South Carolina Historical and Genealogical Magazine* 1, no. 3 (1900): 228–62. http://www.jstor.org/stable/27574919.

Moore, Caroline, ed. *Abstracts of the Wills of the State of South Carolina, 1760–1784.* Vol. 3. Columbia: R.L. Bryan, 1969.

Nichols, Patricia C. *Voices of our Ancestors: Language Contact in Early South Carolina.* Columbia: University of South Carolina Press, 2009.

Nickens, T. Edward. "The Wild Santee." *Garden and Gun* (October/November 2016): 112–21.

Oller, John. *The Swamp Fox: How Francis Marion Saved the American Revolution.* Boston: Da Capo Press, 2016.

Olsberg, R. Nicholas. "Ship Registers in the South Carolina Archives 1734–1780." *The South Carolina Historical Magazine* 74, no. 4 (1973): 189–299. http://www.jstor.org/stable/27567207.

Platt, Steven G., Christopher G. Brantley, and Thomas R. Rainwater. "Native American Ethnobotany of Cane (*Arundinaria spp.*) in the Southeastern United States: A Review." *Castanea* 74, No. 3 (September 2009): 271–85.

Pinckney, Elise, ed. *The Letterbook of Eliza Lucas Pinckney, 1739–1762.* Chapel Hill: University of North Carolina Press, 1972; repr., Columbia: University of South Carolina Press, 1997.

Porcher, Richard D., Jr. "The Vascular Flora of the Francis Beidler Forest in Four Holes Swamp, Berkeley and Dorchester Counties, South Carolina." *Castanea* 46, no. 4 (1981): 248–80. https://www.jstor.org/stable/4032963.

Porcher, Richard D, Jr., and William R. Judd. *The Market Preparation of Carolina Rice: An Illustrated History of Innovations in the Lowcountry Rice Kingdom.* Columbia: University of South Carolina Press, 2014.

Ravenel, Harriott H. *Eliza Pinckney.* New York: Scribner, 1896. Reprinted with the "Journal and Letters of Eliza Lucas." Spartanburg, SC: Reprint Company, 1967.

Raynor, Bob. "Tale of the two great canoeists." *South Carolina Wildlife*, (January/February 2016): 16-21.

Rhode, Fred C., Rudolph G. Arndt, Jeffrey W. Foltz, and Joseph M. Quattro. *Freshwater Fishes of South Carolina.* Columbia: University of South Carolina Press, 2009.

Rogers, George C., Jr. *The History of Georgetown County, South Carolina.* Columbia: University of South Carolina Press, 1970.

Rudes, Blair A. "Place Names of Cofitachequi." *Anthropological Linguistics* 46, no. 4 (Winter 2004): 359–426. http://www.jstor.org/stable/30029015.

Rutledge, Archibald. "Dam Everything." *Field and Stream* (November 1947): 37–8, 116.

—. *God's Children.* Revised edition with foreword by Henry Middleton Rutledge and introduction by Selden B. Hill. Charleston: The History Press, 2009.

—. *Home by the River.* Orangeburg, SC: Sandlapper Publishing, 1983. First published 1941 by Bobbs-Merrill.

—. *The Woods and Wild Things I Remember.* Columbia: R. L. Bryan, 1970.

Ryan, William R. *The World of Thomas Jeremiah: Charles Town on the Eve of the American Revolution.* New York: Oxford University Press, 2010.

Santee Basin Diadromous Fish Restoration Plan, National Marine Fisheries Service (NMFS), North Carolina Wildlife Resources Commission (NMFC), South Carolina Department of Natural Resources (SCDNR), U.S. Fish and Wildlife Service (FWS), 2017.

Savage, Henry, Jr. *River of the Carolinas: The Santee.* New York: Rinehart, 1956.

Savage, Henry, Jr., and Elizabeth J. Savage. *André and Francois Michaux.* Charlottesville: University Press of Virginia, 1986.

Schulz, Constance B. "Eliza Lucas Pinckney and Harriott Pinckney Horry: A South Carolina Revolutionary-Era Mother and Daughter." In *South Carolina Women: Their Lives and Times,* eds. Marjorie J. Spruill, Valinda W. Littlefield, and Joan M. Johnson, vol. 1. Athens: University of Georgia Press, 2009.

Schulz, Constance, ed. *The Papers of Eliza Lucas Pinckney and Harriot Pinckney Horry Digital Edition*. Charlottesville: University of Virginia Press, Rotunda, 2012.

Slocum, Joshua. *Sailing Alone Around the World, and Voyage of the Liberdade*. London: Rupert Hart-Davis Ltd., 1948. *Sailing Alone Around the World* first published 1900, and *Voyage of the Liberdade* first published 1894.

Smith, Hayden R. *Carolina's Golden Fields: Inland Rice Cultivation in the South Carolina Lowcountry, 1670–1860*. Cambridge, UK: Cambridge University Press, 2020.

Sprunt, Alexander, Jr., and E. Burnham Chamberlain. *South Carolina Bird Life*. Columbia: University of South Carolina Press, 1970. Revised edition, with a supplement, E. Milby Burton. First published 1949.

St. James Santee: The Brick Church at Wambaw. St. James Santee Brick Church Restoration Committee. Charleston: Wyrick, 2003.

Stewart, Kevin G., and Mary-Russell Roberson. *Exploring the Geology of the Carolinas: A Field Guide to Favorite Places from Chimney Rock to Charleston*. Chapel Hill: University of North Carolina Press, 2017.

Strickland, John Scott. "'No More Mud Work': The Struggle for the Control of Labor and Production in Low Country South Carolina, 1863–1880." In *The Southern Enigma: Essays on Race, Class, and Folk Culture*. Edited by Walter J. Fraser, Jr. and Winfred B. Moore, Jr. Westport, CT: Greenwood Press, 1983.

Taylor, Emily H. D. "The Draytons of South Carolina and Philadelphia." *Geneaological Society of Pennsylvania* 8, No. 1 (March 1921), 1–26.

Tibbetts, John H. "The Bird Chase." *Coastal Heritage* 15, no. 4 (Spring 2001): 3–13.

Tom Yawkey Wildlife Center. Columbia: South Carolina Department of Natural Resources, 1979.

Turner, Lorenzo D. *Africanisms in the Gullah Dialect*. Chicago: University of Chicago Press, 1949. Reprint, Columbia: University of South Carolina Press, 2001.

Vileisis, Ann. *Discovering the Unknown Landscape: A History of America's Wetlands*. Washington, DC: Island Press, 1997.

Voices of the Santee Delta Oral History Collection. South Carolina Historical Society. The Lowcountry Digital Library. https://lcdl.library.cofc.edu/content/voices-of-the-santee-delta-oral-history-collection.

Waddell, Gene. *Indians of the South Carolina Lowcountry 1562–1751*. Spartanburg, SC: Reprint Company, 1980.

Wallace, David Duncan. *The Life of Henry Laurens*. New York: Russell and Russell, 1915.

Webber, Mabel L. "Dr. John Rutledge and His Descendants." *The South Carolina Historical and Genealogical Magazine* 31, no. 1 (1930): 7–25. http://www.jstor.org/stable/27569816.

Wharton, Charles H., Wiley M. Kitchens, Edward C. Pendleton, and Timothy W. Sipe. *The Ecology of Bottomland Hardwood Swamps of the Southeast: A Community Profile*. U.S. Fish and Wildlife Service, Biological Services Program, Washington, DC, 1982. FWS/OBS-81/37. https://ecos.fws.gov/ServCat/DownloadFile/105358?Reference=65824.

Williams, Roy III, and Alexander Lucas Lofton. *Rice to Ruin: The Jonathan Lucas Family in South Carolina 1783–1929*. Columbia: University of South Carolina Press, 2018.

Willson, Mary F., and Karl C. Halupka. "Anadromous Fish as Keystone Species in Vertebrate Communities." *Conservation Biology* 9, no. 3 (1995): 489–97. http://www.jstor.org/stable/2386604.

Wolff, Geoffrey. *The Hard Way Around: The Passages of Joshua Slocum*. New York: Alfred A. Knopf, 2010.

Wood, Peter H. *Black Majority*. New York: W.W. Norton, 1974.

Wulf, Andrea. *The Brother Gardeners: Botany, Empire, and the Birth of an Obsession*. New York: Vintage Books, 2008.

Young, T. Benton. "Sue Alston: Angel of Hampton Plantation." *Carolana* 2, no. 7 (July 1985), 10, 36, 38.

INDEX

A

A New Voyage to Carolina (Lawson), 70
Aaron (runaway slave), 28, 41-42
Abram (enslaved boatman), 4
ACE Basin, 114
African Methodist Episcopal Church, 55
Alex (ferryman and riverbank builder), 24
Alston, Gerald, 72
Alston, J. Motte, 16-17, 131
Alston, Prince, 74, *74*, 117, 131
Alston, Sue "Ma Dueg," 72-75, *74*, 117, 120, 131
Alston, Will, 131
Amos (enslaved boatman), 27
An Accurate Map of North and South Carolina With Their Indian Frontiers (Mouzon), 42

Anderson family (Murphy Island), 83-84
Annandale Club, 104-5
Annandale Plantation, *23*, 105, 114
Austin, George, 40

B

Baldwin, Bob, 99
Baldwin, William Jr., 105
Ball, Catherine Gendron, 39
Ball, Charles, 29, 85-86
Ball, Elias "Red Cap," 45
Ball, Jane Ball, 45, 48
Ball, John (cousin of "Wambaw Elias"), 45, 48
Ball, John Coming (father of "Wambaw Elias" Ball), 30, 39-40, 41, 43

Ball, John Coming Jr. (half-brother to "Wambaw Elias" Ball), 45, 46
Ball, Judith Boisseau, 39
Ball, "Third Elias," 45, 47
Ball, "Wambaw Elias," 39, 41, 42, 43, 44-48, 86
Bartelme, Tony, 113
Bartram, John, 15, 23
Bartram, William, 6-7, 9, 16, 26
Baruch, Bernard, 131
Batteau (slave of Gov. Bennett), 54
Beidler Forest Sanctuary, 6, 7-8, 123-25, 124
Belmont Plantation, 64, 67
Bennett, Thomas, 51-52, 53, 54
Big Commander Island, 130
Big Patty (enslaved woman), 70
Bishop, Nathaniel Holmes, 77-78, 81-82, 82, 84
Blake's Plantation (Washo), 22, 30, 88, 118
Bowman, John, 30
Brockington and Associates, 11, 43
Brown, Joseph, 41
Brown, Morris, 55
Buchanan, William, 26
Bull, William, 143n
Byrnes, James F., 93-95

C

Cape Island, 78, 80
Cape Romain islands, 99, 119
Cape Romain National Wildlife Refuge, i, 79, 109, 114
Carnes, Henry L., 52
Carney, Judith, 30
Cat Island, 97, 106, 117, 118
Catawba River, 93, 123
Catawba tribe, 3, 12
Catesby, Mark, 9
Cedar Island, 13, 57, 58, 78, 79, 80, 99, 119
Charles Pinckney National Historic Site, 70. *See also* Snee Farm Plantation.

Charleston Harbor, 98, 99
Charleston Navy Base, 98
Church of England, 37
City Gazette, 27, 28, 41
Clark, C.M., 94
Clinton, Henry, 45
Cofitachequi, 3
Collington, Lewis and Abbie Brown, 72
Collins Creek community, 128, 132
Collins, Jonah, 30, 38
Comingtee Plantation, 47
Congaree National Park, 121-23, *122*
Congaree River, 1, 12, 30, 100, 121-23
Constitutional Convention, 141n
Continental Congress, 39, 142n, 143n-144n
Cooper River Rediversion Project, 98-100
Cornwallis, Charles, 45
Crook, Edward, 30
Cudjo (enslaved man), 131
Cuthbert, Edmund A., *95*

D

Daddy Ben (African American mentor), 118
Darling, Jay, 94
Declaration of Independence, 142n
de Ayllón, Lucas Vázquez, 113
de Ecija, Francisco Fernandez, 12
de Soto, Hernando, 12
Dinah (runaway slave), 60
Doar, David, 16
Dollard, Patrick, 46
Dominick, Cecilia and Richard, 118, 128-29
Douglass, Frederick, 60-61
Douxsaint, Paul, 41
Drayton, Charles Sr., 65, 142n, 143n
Drayton, Charlotta Bull, 66, 143n
Drayton, Dorothy Golightly, 63, 65
Drayton Hall, 70-71, 142n
Drayton, Hester Middleton, 63, 65, 142n
Drayton, John Sr., 66, 143n

Drayton, Thomas III, 66
Drayton, William Henry, 65, 143n
Dubose, Samuel, 46
Ducks Unlimited, 113
Duke, James Buchanan, 93
Duke Power Company (Southern Power Company), 93
Dunmore, Lord, 54
DuPont family, 97, 104, 105

E

Echaw Creek, 37
Egerton, John, 74
Eldorado, 117
Endangered Species Act, 94
Evening Post Industries, 114

F

Fairfield Plantation, 30, 31, 65, 88, 125, 130, 127
Federal Power Commission, 97
Ferris, Pat, 97, 118, 152
Finlay, Hugh, 126
Ford, George, 51-52, 54
Francis Marion National Forest, 35-36, 42-43, 114
Fulcher, Jim and family, 73

G

Gaillard, Alcimus, 39
Gaillard, Barthélémy, 3, 8, 39
Gaillard, Elizabeth Serré, 39
Gaillard, John, 45, 47, 48
Gaillard, Lydia Peyre, 39
Gailliard, Peter, 46, 47
Gaillard, Tacitus, 39
Gaillard, Theodore Jr., 39, 45, 48
Gaillard, Theodore Sr., 39, 45, 46
Garden, Hugh R., 105
Gardner, Jeffery, 43
Garrett, George and Celia, 88
Garrett, Johnny, 23, 112

Garrett, Moses, 88
Garrett, William, 22, 23, 88, 105, 112
Gendron, John II, 39
Gendron, Phillipe, 39
Germantown (Germanville), 72, 73, 87, 118, 130-31
Gillings, Seba, 81-82
Giton, Judith, 37
God's Children (Rutledge), 73-74
Gray, John, 41-42
Great Catawba Trading Path, 3
Great Depression, 93, 105
Great Gale of 1822, 4, 56-59, 77, 109
Greater Zion AME Church, 132
Green, Eve Manigault, 18, 128
Green, Sambo, 18, 20, 128, 131, 132

H

Hagley Plantation, 70
Hampton Community Archaeology Project, 71, *71*, 117
Hampton Island, 35, 86
Hampton Plantation, 18, 20, 26, 34, 45, 63-75, *64*, 86, 87, 92, 115, 117, 130, 131
Hampton Plantation State Historic Site, 71, *71*, 74, 114-15, 117
Hannah (enslaved woman), 70
Harrietta Plantation, 116, 130
Harry (enslaved man and spy), 46
Harvey, William S., 52
Hayes, Miles, 8
Hobcaw Barony, 104, 131
Holbrook, Duff, 105
Hollings, Fritz, 98
Home by the River (Rutledge), 92, 115
Hopsewee Plantation, 30, 87, 116, 118, 125
Horry, Daniel Huger, 28, 30, 34, 45, 48, 66-67
Horry, Daniel Huger Jr. (aka Charles Lucas Pinckney Horry), 45, 48, 66-67
Horry, Elias IV, 31, 54

Horry, Elie, 3, 34
Horry, Harriott Pinckney, 4, 27, 28, 45, 57-58, 60, 63-70, 86, 116-17
Horry, Hugh, 45, 48
Horry, Margueritte Huger, 34
Horry, Peter, 27, 45, 46-47, 48
Huger, Daniel (1651-1711), 3, 29, 34, 38, 65, 72
Huger, Daniel (1741-1799), 143n
Huger, Sabina Elliott, 65
Huguenots, 3, 33-34, 37, 38, 39-40, 45, 58, 115
Hume, John, 30
Hurricane Hugo, 43, 58, 109, 124
Hyde Park Plantation, 39
hydroelectric projects, 91, 93-101

I

Ickes, Harold, 94
Incidents in the Life of a Slave Girl (Jacobs), 70
Indian (African American-Indian mentor), 118
indigo cultivation, 40, 67, 68, 69
Izard, Alice DeLancey, 65
Izard, Becky, 68
Izard, Ralph, 65, 143n
Izard, Walter and Elizabeth Gibbes, 65

J

Jack (runaway slave, 1795), 4, 28
Jack (runaway slave from Midlands, 1821), 52
Jack (runaway slave of Mrs. Horry, 1821), 52
Jack Bluff Plantation, 70
James (Henry Laurens's runaway slave), 28, 41-42
Jamestown settlement, 34, 37
Joe (aka Forest, runaway slave, 1821), 51-55, 60-61
John (slave of Elias Horry), 54-55

Johnston, Andrew, 30
Johnstone, Allen, 97-98
Jones, David, 117-18
Jordan, E.D., 87
Joyner, Charles, 131
Judd, William Robert, 19

K

Kjerfve, Björn, 100-101
King Jeremy, 33, 72, 132
King Jeremy's Plantation, 33, 72, 118, 132
Kinloch Gun Club, 97, 105
Kinloch Plantation, *26*, 99, *106*, 113, 114, 117

L

Lake Marion, 60, 95, *95*, 100
Lake Moultrie, 95, 100
Lake Murray, 93
Laurel Hill Plantation, 70
Laurens, Eleanor, 39
Laurens, Henry, 27, 28, 30, 39-43, 46
Laurens, John, 46
Lawson, John, 3, 7, 8, 9, 29, 34, 38
Leland, Jack, 38
Lily Pond Missionary Baptist Church, 128
Limerick Plantation, 143n
Lincoln, Benjamin, 46, 66, 86
Linville Gorge, 123
Lords Proprietors, 34
Lowcountry Land Trust, 113
Lucas family, 72
Lucas, George and Anne Mildrum, 67
Lucas, George Jr., 68
Lucas, Jonathan, 30, 34-35, 129
Lucas, Jonathan Jr., 30
Lucas, William, 30, 35, 129
Lynch, Thomas and Lynch family, 125-26
Lynch's or Lynches Island, 25, 125-128

M

McClellanville, 35, 58
Mace, Bill, 23, 25, 58, 107-8, 109, 110
McGregor, Daniel, 30
Mackenzie, Archibald, 65
Maham, Hezekiah, 46-47
Manigault, Peter, 38, 105, 113, 114
Marion, Elizabeth Gaillard, 39
Marion, Francis, 27, 39, 45, 46-47, 61, 67, 86, 131
Marion, Job, 39, 45
Mathews, John, 65, 143n
Mathews, Mary Wragg, 63, 65
Matthiessen, Evard, 111-12
Matthiessen, Peter, 111-12
Maybank, Burnett, 93, 94-95
Mazyck, Isaac, 3, 30, 131
Mazyck, William, 25-26
Michaux, André, 26
Michel, Jacqueline, 8
Middleton, Arthur M., 65, 142n
Middleton, Esther Mary "Polly" Izard, 63, 65
Middleton, Frances, 30
Middleton, Henry, 65, 66, 142n
Middleton, Mary Mackenzie (Lady Mary), 65, 66
Middleton Place, 142n
Millbrook Plantation, 30, 117
Milligen, George, 31
Mills, Robert, 31
Montgomery Plantation, 131
Morgan, Robert, 42
Morris (former slave at Hobcaw Barony), 131
Motte, Jacob II, 65
Motte, Rebecca Brewton, 65, 117
Moultrie, William, 27, 45, 46
Mouzon, Henry, 42
Murphy Island, 4, 13, 25, 35, 57-59, *59*, 77-84, 98, 107-112, 119, 128

N

National Marine Fisheries Service, 100
National Historic Landmark, 114-15, 116
National Register of Historic Places, 43, 115
Ned (slave of Gov. Bennett), 54
New Deal, 91- 94
North Carolina Wildlife Resources Commission, 100
North Island, 105, 106
North Point Plantation, 72

O

Old Chloe (enslaved woman), 70
Open Space Institute, 130

P

Pardo, Juan, 12
Peachtree Plantation, 30, 125, 130
Pee Dee River, 8, 46
Peterson, Roger Tory, 94
Pinckney, Charles, 66, 67, 68, 69, 141n
Pinckney, Charles Cotesworth, 46, 48, 65, 66, 67, 68, 69, 141n, 143n, 144n
Pinckney, Eliza Lucas, 27, 63, 64, 65, 67-70, 75, 141n
Pinckney, Elizabeth Betsy Motte, 65
Pinckney, Sarah "Sally" Middleton, 63, 65
Pinckney, Thomas, 27, 30, 48, 55, 63-64, 65, 66, 67, 68, 69, 117, 144n
Pinckney, Thomas Jr., 65
Pineville Police Association, 60
Poplin, Eric, 43
Porcher, Richard, 7, 123
Post and Courier, 129
Prevost, Augustine, 63
Prevost, Mike, 114
Pritchard, Gullah Jack, 55

Provincial Congress, 45, 141n, 142n, 143n
Public Works Administration, 93-95, 97

R

Ramsay, David, 68
Ray, Dan, 114
Rattray Green, 41
Ravenel, Harriott Horry, 64, 68
Reconstruction, 24, 78
Redington, Paul G., 94
Revolutionary War:
  Battle of Camden during, 68, 144n
  British defeat during, 47
  British occupation of Charleston during, 27-28, 42, 45-47, 66, 48, 141n, 142n, 144n
  British southern campaign of, 63-64, 66, 86, 144n
  Confiscation Act of 1782 and, 47-48
  effect on Hampton Plantation people of, 63-67
  effect on Wambaw Plantation people of, 44-49
  enslaved people and, 46-47, 54, 56, 63-64
  shifting loyalties during, 45-49, 66-67
rice culture:
  Civil War and, 31, 103
  clearing forests for, 16-18, 17
  decline of, 103, 104
  early years of, 15
  enslaved laborers and, 15-18, 23-24, 30, 31, 40, 103, 131
  freed laborers and, 24, 103
  harvest of, 23
  market preparation of, 30
  reservoir irrigation and, 15, 25, 34
  rice banks and, 22-24
  rice flats and, 25, 26, 28
  rice mills and, 30
  rice trunks and, 18-22, 19, 20, 26, 130, 131
  steam power and, 30
  task system and, 24-25, 70
  tidal irrigation and, iv, 16-22, 77-78
  water-powered mills and, 30, 34, 35
  wealth generated by, 31, 115
Rice Hope Plantation, 30
Richardson, Martha Proctor, 55
Rolla (slave of Gov. Bennett), 54
Romney Plantation, 25, 131
Roosevelt, Franklin Delano, 93, 94
Royal (enslaved man), 60
Rutledge, Archibald, 18, 20, 24, 72, 73-74, 88, 92, 96-97, 115, 130
Rutledge, Edward, 65, 142n
Rutledge, Frederick, 117
Rutledge, John, 46, 67, 142n, 143n
Rutledge, John Jr., 27
Rutledge, Harriott Pinckney Horry, 66, 67, 116-17
Rutledge, Henrietta Middleton, 65

S

Sailing Alone Around the World (Slocum), 82
St. James Brick Church Restoration Committee, 115
St. James Santee (aka "Brick Church"), 37-39, 115, *116*, 131
Sanchez, Ian, 35, 78-80, *79*
Santee Coastal Reserve, 22-23, 58, *89*, 99, 106-9, 113, 117, 118, 128-30
Santee-Cooper Project, 91-101, *85, 96*
  cost of, 95
  damage caused by, 97-100, 119
  environmental impact of, 94-100
  map of, *92*
  opposition to, 93-95, 96-97
  positive impact of, 95-96
  See also Cooper River Rediversion Project
Santee Delta:
  African American people of, 4, 18, 24, 73, 88, 105, 115-20

archaeological sites of, 10-11, *11*, 43, 70-72, 117-8
biting insects of, 4, 18, 26, 109, 110, 113, 126-7, 129, 130
canebrake ecosystem of, 11-12, 52
conservation of, 106-115
damming of rivers in, 91-92, 100. *See also* Santee-Cooper Project.
description of, ii, 2-3, 15
enslaved people of. *See* slavery and enslaved people.
European explorers and settlers of, 3, 12. *See also* Huguenots
ferries on, 25-27
fish of, 14-15, 96-98, 99-100
geology of, 9
hunting preserves in, 87-88, 94, 99, 103-6, *106*, 111-12
indigenous people of, 3, 8, 10-13, 33, 72, 124, 128. *See also* King Jeremy's Plantation, Santee tribe, Sewee tribe
maps of, *iv*, *2*, *44*
prehistoric forest of, 5-8
threats to, 119-20
trees of, 5-8, *6*, 36, 43, 92, 111, 121-25, *122, 124*, 127, *127*
watercraft on, 25-30, *26*, 40, 41, 42, 85, 127
waterfowl and birds of, 15, 36, 94, 99, 103-4, *104*, 107-110, 111-12, 128
waters forming, 1-3, 8, 33, 121, 123. *See also* Congaree River, Santee River, Wateree River, Wambaw Creek
Santee Delta Wildlife Management Area, *104*, 125-28, *127*
Santee Gun Club, 22, 23, 87-88, 94-95, 97, 99, 105-6, *107*, 111-2, 117, 118
Santee River, 5, 8-9, *12*, 93, 121, 123. *See also* Santee-Cooper Project.
North Santee branch of, 9
South Santee branch of, 9, *89*, 114
Santee tribe, 3, 12
Schad, Abraham, 27, 40, 41
Schenck, Rand, 36
Scipio (Seewee Indian), 3, 8
Serré, Noah and Catherine, 30
Sewee tribe, 3, 8-9, 33-34, 72, 118, 132
Singleton, Jimmy, *106*
slavery and enslaved people:
African origins of, 3-4, 17, 24, 28, 40, 119
boatmen among, 27, 29, 41, 42
efforts to control, 26, 54-55, 60
emancipation and, 74, 103
Great Gale of 1822 and, 57-59, 77
Hampton Plantation at, 70-72, 115, 117, 131
languages of, 4
maroon communities and, 53, *53*, 54
Middle Passage and, 4, 18, 28, 119
Negro Seaman Act and, 55
punishment of, 55-56, 60
revolts by, 54-56
Revolutionary War and, 46-47, 54, 56, 63-54
rice production and, 15-31, 40, 77-78, 104, 119, 126
runaways from, 4, 26, 27-28, 51-56, 60-61, 85-86
task system and, 24-25, 70
traders of, 40
value of, 42, 58, 70
Wambaw Plantation at, 39-42
Slocum, Joshua, 77-78, 80, 82-84, *83*
Smalls, Henrietta, 73, 120, 118
Smithsonian Institution, 84
Snee Farm Plantation, 66, 141n. *See also* Charles Pinckney Historic Site.
South Carolina Association, 55
South Carolina Commons House of Assembly (1670-1776), 37, 39, 126, 142n, 143n
South Carolina Department of Natural Resources (formerly South Carolina Wildlife Resources Department), 99, 100, 105, 106-8, 117, 127, 130
South Carolina Gazette, 69

South Carolina General Assembly (1776-present), 46, 47-48, 55, 67, 142n, 143n, 144n
South Carolina Historical Society, ii, 42
South Carolina Public Service Authority, 97. *See also* Santee-Cooper Project.
South Carolina State Parks system, 114-15, 117
South Carolina State Ports Authority, 98
South Island, 6, 15, 22, 51-53, 57, 80, 105, 106
South Island Plantation, 22, 97, 99
South Santee Cemetery, 130, 132
South Santee Senior and Community Center, 128, 132
Still, William, 60
Stono Rebellion, 54
storm towers, 58-59, *59*, 80, 117, 119
Strange, Tommy, 113

T

Tarleton, Banastre, 45, 86, 131
The Nature Conservancy, 106, 111-12, 113, 115, 130
The Oaks Plantation, 142n
Thompson, Benjamin, 47
Tom Yawkey Wildlife Center, 106
Trapier, Paul, 30
Tubman, Harriet, 60
Turnbull, Robert, 55
Turner, Ted, 105, 114

U

United Nations Educational, Scientific and Cultural Organization (UNESCO), 114
U.S. Army Corps of Engineers, 100, 101
U.S. Congress (including House and Senate), 94, 142n, 143n
U.S. Environmental Protection Agency, 94
U.S. Fish and Wildlife Service (formerly Biological Survey), 94, 100
University of South Carolina, 129

V

Vesey, Denmark, 54-55
Village Museum, ii, 35
Voices of the Santee Delta (Raynor), ii-iii, 118, 120
Voyage of the Liberdade (Slocum), 78
Voyage of the Paper Canoe (Bishop), 78

W

Wahaw Creek (aka Hampton Creek), 34
Wambaw (schooner), 30, 40, 41-42
Wambaw Creek, 29, 33-48, *37*, 44
Wambaw Creek Wilderness, 7, 36, 114
Wambaw Plantation (Ball), 4, 27, 28, 39-44, 45, 47
Wambaw Plantation (Horry), 30, 34-36, 45, 70, 72, 74
Wambaw Swamp, 15, 33, 36, 42, 45, 47
Wambaw Swamp Wilderness Area, 44, 114
Wappoo Plantation, 67
Ward, Joshua J., 20-22
Warren, Samuel Fenner, 38
Washington, George, 26, 67, 86, 132, 141n, 144n
Washington, William, 27, 86
Washo Reserve, 106, 111-12, *111*
Watahan Plantation, 12, 29, 34, 38, 72
Wateree River, 1, 3, 15, 53, 60, 93, 121, 123, 143n
Wateree tribe, 14
Web of Water, 78
Wedge Entomological Research Foundation, 129
Wedge Plantation, 35, 117, 119, 128-30
Welch, Don, 98
Westerhold, Jim, 107-8
White Oak Forestry, 114, 130-31

Wilkinson, Phil, 22–23, 58, 87, 99, 105, 116, 118, 127
William (schooner), 56
Williams, Kenny, 99, 105, 113
Williams, Ted, 105
Wineglass, Jane, 18, 118, 128–29, 130, 132, *132*
Winyah Agricultural Society, 20
Woodberry, John, 30
Wood, Peter, 40
Wylie, Walker Gill, 93

Y

Yates, William, 41
Yawkey, Tom, 22, 97, 104, 105, 106. *See also* Tom Yawkey Wildlife Center

Bob Raynor's first book, *Exploring Bull Island: Sailing and Walking Around a South Carolina Sea Island*, published in 2005, combined his interests in adventure, natural history, and the human history of the Lowcountry. In a similar approach, his second work, *Tracing the Cape Romain Archipelago*, expanded his fieldwork and research to the entire Cape Romain area. As part of the research for the current work, Raynor initiated, coordinated, and was the interviewer for the oral history project Voices of The Santee Delta, archived at the Lowcountry Digital Library. He has regularly posted on his blog Raynor on the Coast for over a dozen years "Exploring the Lowcountry and Beyond."

www.ingramcontent.com/pod-product-compliance
Lightning Source LLC
Chambersburg PA
CBHW060157190426
43199CB00044B/2670